THE TRANSFORMATION
OF BRITISH LIFE,
1950–2000

To Paul, Jessica, Matilda,

Saskia, Charlotte and Henry

The transformation of
British life, 1950–2000

A social history

Andrew Rosen

Manchester University Press
Manchester and New York

distributed exclusively in the USA by Palgrave

Published by Manchester University Press
Oxford Road, Manchester M13 9NR, UK
and Room 400, 175 Fifth Avenue, New York, NY 10010, USA
www.manchesteruniversitypress.co.uk

Distributed exclusively in the USA by
Palgrave, 175 Fifth Avenue, New York NY 10010, USA

Distributed exclusively in Canada by
UBC Press, University of British Columbia, 2029 West Mall,
Vancouver, BC, Canada V6T 1Z2

British Library Cataloguing-in-Publication Data
A catalogue record for this book is available from the British Library

Library of Congress Cataloging-in-Publication Data
A catalog record for this book is available from the Library of Congress

ISBN 13: 978-0-7190-6612-2

First published by Manchester University Press 2003

First digital paperback edition published 2008

Printed by Lightning Source

Contents

Figures

Tables

Preface

In this book I will argue that during the second half of the twentieth century, life in Britain altered so greatly as to have been transformed. The period saw radical changes in some of the most fundamental aspects of people's lives, including housing, food, transport, religion, education and employment. This book examines the diverse developments which so altered British life.

The idea that life in Britain has been transformed is hardly new – for example, in *British Society Since 1945*, first published in 1982 and probably the most widely-read of the social histories which deal with the post-war period, Arthur Marwick referred to the 'profound developments – particularly growing spending power in all sections of society ... which were to bring about a transformation in British social life'.[1] Similarly, in an article published in 1994 Edward Royle referred to the 'massive transformation of society' which had taken place in the last forty to forty-five years.[2] It is hard to imagine that any social historian would look at the second half of the twentieth century without considering the enormous improvement in standards of living or major changes in gender roles, to cite but two examples. A great deal remains to be investigated, however, including not only the nature of many kinds of social and attitudinal change but possible links or similarities between seemingly disparate developments. This book explores how life changed, why changes took the form they did and the nature of the relationships between those changes.

The topic of this book has been refined during the course of seven years of research and writing. One choice which had to be made early on was whether to consider life in England alone or in Britain as a whole. There were arguments for both approaches. On the one hand, almost seven times as many people live in England as in Scotland and Wales combined – by 2000 there were 49,997,000 people in England as opposed to only 5,115,000 in Scotland and 2,946,000 in Wales.[3] The marked imbalance between those populations means that numerical statements about Britain as a whole do not necessarily reflect conditions in Scotland or Wales. On the other hand, it quickly became clear that almost all of the published statistics which would be needed for this book represented either the United Kingdom or Great Britain or England and Wales combined so that it would be impractical to attempt to portray English realities alone. Moreover, doing so would give the work a parochial quality which I wished to avoid. I therefore decided to consider Great Britain as a whole, the one exception being a few pages in the introduction in which a largely English focus seemed appropriate. Throughout the rest of the book, Wales and Scotland have been included to the extent that they are naturally represented by statistics about Great Britain, but they have not been discussed or analysed as separate entities in their own right. Similarly, Northern Ireland has for the most part been considered only to the extent that it is included in statistics describing the United Kingdom, although the unusual role of religion in Northern Ireland is discussed in the chapter on religion.

In planning this book, it was also necessary to decide whether to opt for a topical or chronological approach. Either format would have distinct advantages and disadvantages. I eventually decided to discuss one topic (or several related topics) in each chapter so that it would be possible to consider each topic as a historical entity. Each chapter would cover the same historical period so the chapters could hardly be arranged in chronological order. I decided to arrange them in relation to what seemed to me to be the most important themes of the period. This book contains thirteen chapters which have been organised under four headings: Part I, 'Standards of living, qualities of life', examines the enormous rise in standards of living which took place between 1950 and 2000 and goes on to investigate how the economic pie was sliced by

region and by social class. Part II, 'Orthodoxies in decline', dis-
cusses the major loss of popular support for the monarchy, religion, marriage and the trade unions which took place between
1950 and 2000. Part III, 'New opportunities, new roles', examines
the widespread changes in education which helped to make it possible for women and members of ethnic minorities to play new
roles. The changing character of youth and age are also analysed
in Part III. Finally, Part IV, 'Redefining Britain', explores three
developments which are not usually considered by social historians, namely the profound influence on British life of the international style of architecture, American culture and Britain's
ever-growing involvement with European institutions. The transformation of British life has not occurred in a vacuum, and major
developments in the outside world have had a far greater impact
than some social historians suggest.

With regard to the period covered by this book, I chose 1950
as a starting date for two reasons. Aside from the fact that 1950
was the century's mid-point, I wanted to exclude from detailed
consideration the period of austerity which followed the war.
Austerity gradually came to an end during the early 1950s, a
decade which in many ways was a period of gestation and therefore seemed a good place to begin. After the early 1950s Britain
experienced a phenomenal growth of prosperity which made life
very different from what it had been before, during or just after the
war. Many of the developments discussed in this book had pre-war
roots, but with a few exceptions I have resisted the temptation to
explore those roots in any detail as doing so would alter the focus
of the book.

I am deeply grateful to the colleagues and friends who read parts of
the draft manuscript of this book and provided me with criticism
and advice. Paul Addison, Muriel Burton, Dana Greene, Fred
Leventhal, Arthur Marwick, Geoffrey Tyack and Chris Waters all
gave me many invaluable suggestions. An entire chapter of this book
would not exist if Fred Leventhal had not suggested that I write it.

I would also like to thank Sian Crisp, Verity Mason and Rob Murison for their thoughtful comments. I am particularly indebted to my wife Adrienne, who gave me the benefit of her considerable historical and editorial expertise and my son Paul and Gina Bateson who helped to edit the manuscript for publication.

I would also like to thank various members of the staff of the Bodleian Library as well as the staffs of the Geography, Social Sciences, Education, Economics and Law Libraries of Oxford University. Almost all of the research and writing of this book was carried out in one or another of those libraries. Christine Mason, David Busby, Helen Rogers and Vera Ryhajlo were all very helpful over a number of years.

Finally, the staff of the Manchester University Press have provided unstinting support at all stages of this project. One could not ask for a more helpful publisher.

Introduction

Britain is an island, surrounded by cold seas. Over the centuries it has become the home of a society which recognises many boundaries – tangible boundaries between places and intangible boundaries between people. The great primal boundary has always been the sea itself. For hundreds of years the sea served as a barrier against invasion from abroad. Spain, France, and Ireland were all potential (and, occasionally, actual) enemies. Within Britain, as centuries passed, boundaries of many kinds increasingly structured national, regional and local life. The medieval city walled out the savage countryside and individual edifices such as castles and colleges walled out the stranger. The cathedral close formed another barrier, protecting prayer from the tumult of the workaday world. A network of intangible boundaries also emerged as Britons developed complex structures of land ownership, rank and social class, assigning to men and women roles inherited by birth which markedly defined their lives.

Down the centuries much has changed, but intricate structures derived from historical precedent remain particularly important in Britain. The gradual evolution of Britain's democratic institutions has long been a source of great pride, but Britain has also retained the world's wealthiest and most highly-publicised monarchy and the unelected House of Lords. On 24 November 1998, the government announced in the Queen's Speech that 'a Bill will be introduced to remove the right of hereditary peers to sit and vote in the House of Lords'.[1] Arguably the most noteworthy thing about this announcement was that it was not made until almost the end of the twentieth century. Would any other major western industrialised democracy have waited so long to take such a step?

Until almost the end of the twentieth century, the Lords as well as the monarchy remained potent symbols of the continuing importance of inherited privilege in British life. As David Cannadine has observed, 'Britain retains intact an elaborate, formal system of rank and precedence, culminating in the monarchy itself, which means that prestige and honour can be transmitted and inherited across the generations.'[2] Hierarchical patterns have also survived in the remarkably disproportionate role played by former pupils of the most prestigious independent schools and graduates of Oxford and Cambridge in running the nation's public affairs, particularly when the Conservatives have been in office. At the end of the Major government in 1997, 18 out of the 23 Cabinet ministers had been educated at independent schools. In 1995 almost half of the Conservative Members of Parliament (149 MPs out of 319) were graduates of Oxford or Cambridge, as were 17 out of the then 22 Cabinet members.[3] Moreover, 17 out of the 19 Law Lords had studied at either Oxford or Cambridge.[4] Of broader significance, of the 909 senior civil servants and other top officials in government employment whose education was described in *The Whitehall Companion 1997–98*, 373 or 41 per cent had received degrees from either Oxford or Cambridge, as had 11 out of the 18 Permanent Secretaries.[5] In no other major democracy do the graduates of just two institutions play such a prominent role in shaping national policy, although the extent of that role has diminished somewhat with Labour in office. Moreover, the social background as well as the gender representation of Oxford and Cambridge undergraduates has changed considerably since 1950.

While many of those who occupy high positions still share a common educational background, emphasising one phenomenon alone would distort a far more complex picture. Britain has often been described as a society preoccupied with class. In *The Lion and the Unicorn* (1941), George Orwell claimed that England was 'the most class-ridden country under the sun'.[6] Orwell's oft-quoted phrase has not lacked counterparts down the years, for as A. H. Halsey has commented, 'a class-ridden society' has been 'the common judgement on Britain made by social observers'.[7] For example, Ken Young has written that 'social class divisions are by no means as fluid as is sometimes thought. Rather, class appears to be a pervasive, persistent and immutable feature of British social life'.[8] Class suggests vertical stratification along lines such as upper, middle, and lower class or the more highly segmented models used by sociologists and statisticians. These models are usually determined by occupation alone. For example, the Registrar General's Social Class Scale consists of professional, managerial and technical, non-manual skilled, manual skilled, partly skilled and unskilled workers. Such models have the virtues of clarity and verifiability, but for certain purposes a richer and more nuanced if less easily described and measured picture can be obtained from the broader concept of classification. Despite numerous and unceasing permutations, British society resembles a large multi-segmented honeycomb, the occupants of which are apt to regard each other as inhabiting specific cells, such as Cockneys, country gentlemen, university graduates and so on. To be identified as belonging to a social, educational and organizational cell can be of singular importance. It provides friends, an identity, and a way of life. To be a graduate of one of the great public schools is to possess an ineradicable identity. For Britons, membership really counts, whether it is membership of a college, a regiment, or a trade union. It is arguable that memberships of many kinds form the building blocks of a free society, the little platoons which collectively form a bulwark against totalitarian forms of rule. Personal identity derives, however, from far more than institutional affiliations alone.

Britons initially convey personal identity primarily by speech, which is the most obvious hallmark of social class. Accent, vocabulary, tone, and turns of phrase all count. Speech is important partly because the sound and content of British speech vary so greatly according to class, education and region. A wealth of regional accents, expressions and identities have been preserved by the fact that Britons are not particularly peripatetic as far as long-term residence is concerned. Moves from one residence to another within the same locality are common, with about one-third of all families moving house every five years, but long-distance moves occur much less often. In response to a question asked by a MORI poll, 'Have you always lived within about ten miles of here, or have you ever lived somewhere else?' almost half of the respondents (48 per cent) replied that they had always lived within about ten miles.[9] Calculation of the annual movement of National Health Service doctors' patients between Family Health Service authorities in 2000 indicated that about 1,349,000 people moved to new regions, which was less than 2 per cent of the total population of the UK.[10] And research by Barry McCormick has indicated that manual workers in the United States are eighteen times more likely to move between regions than British manual workers.[11]

Social class is of course not just a matter of speech. In three fairly recent studies, Britons listed the most important criteria of social class as the way people speak (33 per cent), where people live (28 per cent), the friends they have (27 per cent), their job (22 per cent), the sort of school they went to (21 per cent), the way they spend their money (18 per cent), the way they dress (12 per cent) and the car they own (5 per cent).[12] What is particularly significant is not the relative importance attached to different signs of social class so much as the general agreement that class matters greatly in British life. In surveys completed in 1991, fully 74 per cent of respondents believed that social class affects a person's opportunities in Britain either 'a great deal' (27 per cent) or 'quite a lot' (47 per cent), 59 per cent of respondents believed that 'if you want to get ahead it is important to talk with the right accent' and 76 per cent believed that Britain has 'too many barriers based on social class'.[13] Britons were thus well aware of the degree of social segmentation which their ways of speaking represented. As A. H. Halsey has observed, 'no one could grow up in England without acquiring a deep personal-cum-anthropological knowledge of class and status'.[14]

From birth to death, class has a profound influence on Britons' lives. If class is defined by occupation on a six-class scale, men in the top class (professionals) have a life expectancy at birth 7.4 years longer than men in the bottom class (unskilled labourers). Women in the top class have a life expectancy 5.7 years longer than women in the bottom class.[15] Men and women in the two top classes are about three centimetres taller than men and women in the two bottom classes.[16] Members of unskilled manual labourers' households are three times as likely to have a chronic illness as members of professional households.[17] Men and women in the bottom class are also far more likely to be unemployed; throughout the 1990s manual labourers were about three times as likely to be unemployed as professionals.[18] Class also has a profound effect on Britons' chances of entering higher education. Sixteen-year-olds with at least one parent with a university degree are more than twice as likely to take AS and A level examinations leading to university entrance as 16-year-olds with no parent who is a university graduate.[19]

While class perpetuates gross inequalities, it also provides a basis for shared loyalties. These are expressed in many different ways. To belong to the Transport and General Workers Union or another trade union is to share a common bond. The British Medical Association represents doctors just as other associations speak for those who practise other professions. Newspapers too speak for class-based affinity groups. Advertisements for teachers and social workers usually appear in the *Guardian* because teachers and social workers are apt to read the *Guardian*, which supports the interests of public-sector employees. In contrast, *The Times*, with its habitual respect for the great and the good, speaks for what used to be called the establishment. *The Times* caters to a distinctly up-market clientele, but News International, which publishes *The Times*, also publishes the tabloid *Sun*, which addresses a mass-market audience in considerably less dulcet tones. The *Sun* has by far the largest circulation of any newspaper in Britain.

For better or worse, class-based affinities make a major contribution to the continuity of British life. Yet continuity is also rooted in habits and beliefs which are not class-based. Most Britons believe in parliamentary democracy, the importance of due process and the right to freedom of speech, all of which are deeply embedded in law and custom. It is, after all, hard to imagine Britons voluntarily abandoning multi-party democracy. At a more mundane level, national habits such as the propensity to form a queue on the slightest pretext also have little to do with social class. Similarly, much-loved pastimes such as gardening are enjoyed by all classes. Briton never was a nation of shopkeepers but it really is a nation of gardeners. About half of all adult Britons participate in some form of gardening – for about four hours per week on average – and thirty-five million rose bushes are sold in Britain every year.[20] In addition, a strikingly high proportion of Britons visit stately homes and gardens, formerly the private domains of the wealthy alone. According to a MORI survey of 1,230 British adults, within twelve months 39 per cent visited a National Trust house and garden whereas only 19 per cent went to a football match and only 17 per cent attended a pop concert.[21] It is hardly a coincidence that the National Trust with its strong rural and historic bias has become Britain's largest charity by far, with 2,758,250 members at the end of 2000.[22]

For centuries, gardens and old houses have been particularly important facets of country life. Thousands of picturesque villages evoke a seemingly timeless world of cottages, cricket and summer fetes, a world which has often been seen as quintessentially English. In his influential (if controversial) book, *English Culture and the Decline of the Industrial Spirit, 1850–1980,* Martin Wiener argued that by the end of the nineteenth century 'an "English way of life" was defined and widely accepted; it stressed nonindustrial noninnovative and nonmaterial qualities, best encapsulated in rustic imagery – "England is the country", in Stanley Baldwin's phrase ... This countryside of the mind was everything industrial society was not – ancient, slow-moving, stable, cosy, and "spiritual".'[23] Ancient cathedrals, market towns and rural lanes were the real England. England was Hardy and Elgar and *The Wind in the Willows.* This romantic vision was not so much inaccurate as highly selective. It ignored the fact that most farm labourers lived in grinding poverty not to mention the fact that the majority of English people actually lived either in urban slums or anonymous suburbs.

The great majority of Britons do not own historic country or village properties. For that majority the continuity and stability of British life have long been rooted not in rural aspirations but in profound respect for a wide array of established practices and institutions. One of the main concerns of this book is the remarkable extent to which that respect has weakened since 1950. During the first half of the twentieth century, the police, the monarchy, the churches and marriage itself were all regarded as worthy and venerable institutions, fair game for the occasional grumble or affectionate jibe but rarely the subjects of widespread and prolonged disaffection. In contrast, it is striking just how much erosion of confidence in these and other important institutions (such as the trade unions) took place during the second half of the twentieth century. In considering attitudinal change of this ilk one must be careful not to oversimplify. To long for a golden age, a vanished world which was safe and cosy and filled with certainty, is an all-too-common human propensity. It is easy to gild in retrospect a past which did not seem so golden at the time. Yet it would be hard to deny that the rates of drug addiction and recorded crime rose greatly during the second half of the twentieth century or that the rates of divorce and single parenthood rose rapidly as well.

For the purposes of this book, it would be misleading to consider such changes outside the context of two of the most important transformations of British life of the post-war era – the growth of a far higher standard of living and the opening up of a wide array of individual freedoms. Between 1950 and 2000, greatly increased standards of living came to provide most Britons with choices of housing, entertainment, food and travel beyond the dreams of earlier generations. The myriad choices afforded by affluence combined with greatly enlarged personal freedoms to transform lives and aspirations. One result was that changes in values and practices blurred or obliterated many of the stereotypes and rigid conventions which once stifled so many lives. Who would disagree with the proposition that British life has become much less hide-bound than it was in 1950? Not many thoughtful women, surely, nor many homosexuals. And the ubiquitous television interview has made it impossible for governments to be nearly as secretive as they were before the war. A wide variety of attitudinal change would not have been possible without the remarkable growth in standards of living (which, among other things, placed a colour television in almost every household), so I will first explore changes in standards of living before going on to examine the decline of various orthodoxies which has made it possible for Britain to become a far more flexible and diverse society.

Part I

*Standards of living,
qualities of life*

1

In prosperous times

During the second half of the twentieth century standards of living rose remarkably in all of the industrialised democracies. The United Kingdom was no exception. Yet for many decades the sense of well-being which resulted from Britain's increased prosperity was tempered by a realisation that the country was failing to keep economic pace with its competitors. The simultaneous development of these two factors, a phenomenal long-term rise in the standard of living combined with long-term economic growth weaker than that of competing nations, resulted in a paradox of singular importance. Since the war, average income has grown faster than in any period since the industrial revolution, yet for much of that period the rate of growth of Britain's per capita gross domestic product remained consistently lower than that of its economic rivals.

Popular concern with national decline began to increase after the Suez crisis of 1956. The sense of decline took various forms, from nostalgia for imperial power to fear of American cultural influence to widespread belief that an inefficient British economy was being stifled by inept management and rigid trade union practices. Worries about the health of the economy began in the late 1950s and became much stronger during the 1960s. Britain's rate of economic growth reached record heights during the three decades after 1950, but it was during those same decades that the largest gap opened between Britain's rate of economic expansion and that of its main rivals. Manufacturing became the focus of anxiety as Britain experienced a continuing fall in its share of world trade in manufactured products. That share had reached 30 per cent during the export drive shortly after the war but fell to 25 per cent by 1950, 14 per cent by 1964, and under 8 per cent by the early 1980s. Between

1978 and 2000, the proportion of the British labour force employed in manufacturing fell from 31 per cent to 17 per cent whereas the proportion of the labour force employed in the service sector rose from 69 per cent to 83 per cent.[1]

In view of the pervasive shift from industry to services, it became increasingly unclear whether the quasi-permanent price would be a painfully large number of unemployed, a structural (rather than cyclical) problem caused by what came to be called deindustrialisation. The question remains unresolved. Some experts have argued that a substantial shift from industry to services becomes inevitable in maturing economies and that countries with such economies should attempt to build up their service sectors to offset the irreversible trend.[2] The case is arguable, but what actually happened in Britain between 1950 and 2000 was that deindustrialisation was accompanied by increasingly high unemployment. Unemployment averaged only 1.67 per cent during the 1950s, 2.03 per cent during the 1960s, and 4.31 per cent during the 1970s, rising to 5.7 per cent by 1979.[3] Unemployment figures for the 1980s and 1990s were not strictly comparable with those of earlier decades, but the relatively high level was clear, unemployment rates adjusted to ILO specifications being 9.8 per cent in 1981, 8.8 per cent in 1991 and 5.3 per cent in the autumn of 2000.[4] The problem was hardly Britain's alone; by 2000 most of the major European economies had substantially higher unemployment than Britain.

Given the emergence of unemployment as a serious long-term problem, in examining the unprecedented rise in standards of living which occurred between 1950 and 2000 it is essential to distinguish between averages based on the population as a whole and the condition of specific groups such as the unemployed or elderly people on fixed incomes. The fact that more and more people prospered is not to say that everyone did, although it seems appropriate to consider the population as a whole before going on to consider those who did not receive an equal slice of the pie.

Houses and possessions

During the second half of the twentieth century the standard of living for most Britons rose a great deal. Between 1971 and 2000 alone household disposable income per head doubled, reaching its highest point in history.[5] As to what people did with their new spending power, by far the largest investment of the majority of families was the purchase of a home. Partly as a result of the policies of the Thatcher government, by 2000 more than twice as many dwellings were owned by their occupants as in 1961.[6] This was, however, only the most recent phase of the long-term trend in which the percentage of owner-occupied dwellings rose from 10 per cent in 1914 to 69 per cent by 2000.[7] The change was not just a matter of ownership, but of living conditions as well. In 1951 over 37 per cent of British households had neither a bath nor a shower, but by 1991 fewer than 1 per cent lacked such fundamental amenities. As recently as 1961, 22 per cent of households had no hot water tap, but by 1991 virtually all households had one. Particularly important, in 1964 only about 8 per cent of British households had central heating, but by 2000, 91 per cent of households had it.[8] Yesterday's luxury became today's necessity, and houses became not only warmer but cleaner in the absence of soot from open fires.

As Britain changed from being a nation in which the majority of people lived in unevenly-heated rented accommodation to a nation in which the majority owned centrally-heated homes, those homes came to contain an ever-widening variety of possessions. Increased prosperity fostered one new consumer product after another, and technological advances (such as transistors) and efficiencies of scale in both manufacturing and retailing led to marked reductions in the prices of many durable goods. The result was not only substantial growth in the ownership of familiar appliances such as telephones, refrigerators and washing machines – which only a minority had possessed before the war – but massive sales of newly-developed products such as televisions, stereos and long-playing records, later to be followed by videos, compact discs, computers and mobile phones. The degree and rapidity of change were striking. In 1956 only 8 per cent of British households had refrigerators and as recently as the 1960s the majority of British households did not possess telephones or cars and only slightly more than half had washing machines (see table 1.1).

Table 1.1
Percentage of households with selected durable goods, 1964–65 to 1999–2000, UK

	1964/65	1999/2000
Telephone	22	95
Refrigerator/freezer	38	99
Car or van	38	71
Washing machine	55	91

Sources: S. Toland, 'Changes in Living Standards since the 1950s', *Social Trends 1980* (London: CSO, HMSO, 1980), p. 32, *Abstract of Regional Statistics*, no. 3 (London: HMSO, 1967), Table 49, p. 57 and *Annual Abstract of Statistics, 2001* (London: ONS, SO, 2001), Table 8.4, p. 122.

By 2000 most households had not only a telephone, refrigerator and washing machine but a variety of devices which did not even exist thirty years earlier – 86 per cent of households had video recorders, 80 per cent had microwave ovens, 72 per cent had compact disc players and 44 per cent had at least one mobile phone. The most influential and time-consuming addition to the British home was, however, the television set. Televisions were still an exotic curiosity soon after the war but had become a normal part of virtually every household fifty years later. By 2000 over 99 per cent of British households had televisions, almost all of which were colour sets.[9]

Taken as a whole, new possessions profoundly affected the forms of communication, entertainment, food and transport. The prodigious increase in the number of private telephones, radios and televisions greatly increased the variety and quantity of information entering the home. The telephone and its recent permutation, the mobile phone, made it possible to talk to almost anyone, anywhere, at any time. Television, in turn, gave virtually every adult an unparalleled opportunity to see the world at first hand. In September 1938 Neville Chamberlain could describe the crisis in Czechoslovakia as 'a quarrel in a far-away country between people of whom we know nothing.'[10] By the spring of 1999 no one would have used such words to describe ethnic cleansing in Kosovo. Year after year, television documentaries illuminated the darker corners of the world.

On a less sombre note, television provided endless entertainment, some of which was of admirable quality. From *The Singing Detective* to *Wallace and Gromit*, British television could surprise and delight. In a more elegiac mode, *Brideshead Revisited* used Castle Howard as an elegant setting in which to portray Evelyn Waugh's eccentric aristocrats in inexorable decline. In contrast, *EastEnders* and *Coronation Street* portrayed the vicissitudes of working-class life. In a lighter vein, from Tony Hancock to Peter Cook to the Pythons to Stephen Fry, Rowan Atkinson, Lenny Henry, Victoria Wood, Eddie Izzard and many others, gifted comedians gave Britons a unique opportunity to laugh at themselves.

On the other hand, at least two negative consequences also flowed from the ubiquitous box. First, almost every evening millions of Britons watched fictional characters being beaten, stabbed and shot. Any number of violent acts were portrayed every week in the name of entertainment. No one was sure of the consequences, but it was possible that one result was a desensitisation to the pain and grief caused by real violence and a more ready acceptance of violence as a normal part of life. Second, watching television required physical inertia on the part of the viewer. For many children the combination of extensive television viewing and the playing of computer games meant that hour after hour was spent sitting indoors which could have been spent in active outdoor pursuits. In 2000 the average adult in the UK watched television for about 27 hours per week and the average child between 4 and 15 watched for about 18 hours per week.[11] It was not entirely coincidental that obesity had become a national problem.

Entertainment in the home was also transformed by vast improvements in the sound of music. During the 1950s and 1960s, long-playing records and stereos made possible substantial refinements in the fidelity of music reproduction systems. Later the tape deck was followed by the compact disc, 176 million of which were sold in the UK in 1999.[12] An extraordinary outpouring of popular music was made possible by the post-war boom in teenagers' power to purchase records, tapes and compact discs. Moreover, the advent of central heating and warmer houses made it possible for teenagers to turn their bedrooms into living rooms replete with gear which no teenager could possibly have possessed before the war. By 1996 eight out of ten 15 to 19-year-olds had a television in their bedroom.[13] The many-faceted youth culture which first emerged during the 1950s will be discussed in detail in Chapter 10.

Food

The second half of the twentieth century not only saw major developments in communication and entertainment but also witnessed nothing less than a revolution in the quality and character of British food. Few under forty could fully appreciate just how bland and unimaginative most British food was before the mid-1950s. The revolution in what Britons ate and where they ate it had at least eight intertwined roots – the end of rationing, post-war prosperity, the work of pioneers such as Elizabeth David and Raymond Postgate, substantial immigration to Britain from Commonwealth countries, much-increased British travel abroad, unprecedented advances in food preservation, substantial growth in the number of married women working outside the home and the growth of popular understanding of dietary needs.

The late Christopher Driver, who edited the *Good Food Guide* from 1969 to 1982, wrote that 'compared with France, regionalism in the production of specialities and in the palate for distinctive local foods is not pronounced in Britain' and that 'historically ... differentiation in British food culture has been determined by social hierarchy rather than by regional geography'.[14] In other words, class rather than region has been the primary determinant of what Britons eat. The difference has been not just a matter of taste but of nutrition. In 1914 most Britons were still so poorly fed that the rations of millions who served in the war provided better nourishment than they had ever known before.[15] The nourishment gap continued during the inter-war years – in 1936-37 the difference between the richest and poorest groups was 40 per cent for calorie intake, 71 per cent for vitamin B_1 and 81 per cent for vitamin A.[16] Like much else, nutrition was largely a matter of which compartment one found oneself travelling in.

Country house and Mayfair culinary marathons aside, most Britons' diet before the war was remarkably dull. The American writer Mary Ellen Chase, who studied at Cambridge for two years, wrote in 1936,

> This suspicion of superfluous emotion, of all manner of excess, is clearly evident in the Englishman at his table. He does not want his meat served up with sauces that disguise its taste, seeing in this a violation against the nature, the honest character of what he is eating. He has no fondness for dressed-up, flighty foods, dislikes fancy ices, intricate salads, unfamiliar sweets. He knows where he is when he is eating gooseberry tart, treacle sponge, and suet pudding; and he likes to know where he is. Garnishes, condiments, flavourings, spices, relishes, appetizers – these seem to him unnecessary and excessive, especially when they disguise his fare.[17]

Lacking the complexity and sophistication of so much French and Italian cooking, pre-war British food was apt to involve minor variations on a theme of plainly-cooked meat, potatoes, boiled vegetables and conventional puddings, at least for those who could afford to eat relatively well.

During the war years, rationing restricted the amount of food Britons could purchase for home preparation or eat in restaurants. Moreover, shipping was badly disrupted and many foods were either rare or unavailable. After the war, poor harvests, world food shortages and the end of lend-lease led to rationing becoming more severe. The meat ration was reduced from war-time levels and bread was rationed from 1946 to 1948. In 1948 the weekly ration for a man was 13 ounces of meat, 8 ounces of sugar, 6 ounces of butter or margarine, 2 pints of milk, 1.5 ounces of cheese, 1 ounce of cooking fat and 1 egg. Obviously, major culinary change had to await the end of food shortages and rationing, both of which slowly drew to a close between 1948 and 1953. As late as the early 1950s tinned fruit was still virtually unobtainable in some parts of Britain.[18]

Five years after the end of the war the food revolution began. The year 1950 was the *annus mirabilis* which saw the publication of Elizabeth David's first volume, *A Book of Mediterranean Food*, Raymond Postgate's founding of the Good Food Club and the lifting of most of the rationing restrictions applicable to hotels and restaurants. As a young upper-class bohemian, Elizabeth David had lived for years in France, Italy, Greece, Egypt and India before returning to England in 1946. Her first book opened with a clarion call to the palate:

> The cooking of the Mediterranean shores, endowed with all the natural resources, the colour and flavour of the south, is a blend of tradition and brilliant improvisation. The Latin genius flashes from the kitchen pans ... The ever-recurring elements in the food throughout these countries are the oil, the saffron, the garlic, the pungent local wines; the aromatic perfume of rosemary, wild marjoram and basil drying in the kitchens; the brilliance of the market stalls piled high with pimentos, aubergines, tomatoes, olives, melons, figs and limes; the great heaps of shiny fish, silver, vermilion or tiger-striped, and those long needle fish whose bones mysteriously turn green when they are cooked.[19]

Neither the colours nor the flavours nor the ambience were English in the slightest. *Mediterranean Food* was soon followed by *French Country Cooking* (1951), *Italian Food* (1954) and other volumes which captured the allure of European and Mediterranean cuisine. The food which David described with such brio was, in her own words, 'over-picturesque, perhaps, for every day; but then who wants to eat the same food every day?'[20] The ingredients were intended, she later added, 'to make up what is so often lacking in English cooking: variety of flavour and colour, and the warm, rich, stimulating smells of genuine food.'[21] Elizabeth David's books were to become the Bible of the food revolution.

British food had long been dull not only because of limited culinary knowledge and technique but because of the scarcity of discerning eaters. The founding of the Good Food Club in 1950 by Raymond Postgate, who was already well-known as a historian and journalist, led to the publication of the first edition of *The Good Food Guide* in 1951. The *Guide* was not designed to be a forum for experts – Postgate, a socialist, based his publication on ordinary readers' evaluations of restaurants' food and service. This, he realised, would require a new attitude towards dining out: 'On sitting down at the table polish the cutlery and glasses with your napkin. Don't do this ostentatiously or with an annoyed expression, do it casually. You wish to give the impression not that you are angry with this particular restaurant, but that you are suspicious, after a lifetime of suffering.'[22] By successfully involving his readers and inviting their forthright criticisms, Postgate did a great deal to encourage the growth of a far more discerning attitude towards restaurant food. The history of the *Guide* cannot be explored here, but it is interesting to note that of the 484 restaurants, pubs and hotels serving food outside London described in the first edition of 1951, only eleven were primarily dedicated to serving foreign food and those eleven were almost entirely European in character, there being only one Asian restaurant (Chinese) included.[23]

The ground-breaking innovations of the 1950s did not bring about widespread results until the prosperity and innovative spirit of the 1960s. What took place during that decade was not primarily a revival of traditional British cooking – though important elements of revival were certainly present – but a wholesale broadening of British tastes (or, at least, middle-class tastes) in which the most important element was an ever-increasing variety of foreign food. This trend could not have reached the proportions it eventually did without the substantial increase in Commonwealth immigration into Britain. Between 1951 and 1971 the number of members of ethnic minorities resident in the UK rose at least ten-fold.[24] Post-war immigration had major consequences for British society, most of which will be discussed in Chapter 8. The one by-product of immigration relevant to this chapter was the opening of more and more foreign restaurants. By 1970 there were 4,000 Chinese catering businesses in the UK despite there being modest numbers of Chinese. In the early 1960s there were only about 100 Indian restaurants in the UK, but by 1995 there were about 10,000 Indian restaurants which employed between 60,000 and 70,000 people and had a turnover of £1.5 billion per year, more than coal, steel and shipbuilding combined.[25]

Britons were also exposed to foreign food by travel abroad. With the growth of post-war prosperity foreign travel boomed. The number of foreign holidays taken by Britons rose from about four million in 1965 to about thirty-seven million by 2000; by 2000 foreign holidays represented more than half of all holidays taken and more than eight out of ten British adults had been abroad.[26] Greatly-increased foreign travel as well as ever more foreign restaurants in the UK introduced foreign dishes to millions of Britons, and one result was that formerly exotic food became more and more welcome in British homes, particularly in the form of preprepared frozen and chill-cooked dishes which eliminated the need to search out unfamiliar ingredients or learn what to do with them. By the 1990s supermarkets were selling a wide array of frozen foreign food, from chicken korma to lamb pasanda to pasta penne nicoise to tagliatelle carbonara to premium-priced American ice creams. Sales in the UK of Indian ready-made meals and snacks reached £331 million in 1997.[27] Towards the end of its life even British Rail, hardly the home of gastronomic invention, was offering microwaved chicken tikka masala and thai-style vegetables in its buffet cars, an option which would have been unthinkable forty years earlier. Subsequently, the newly-privatised rail companies continued to offer similar fare. In a similar vein, BP service station takeaway counters took to offering Goan-style prawn naan as well as cappuccino.

The enormous increase in the home consumption of foreign food would have been impossible without the development of the frozen food industry. Home consumption of frozen food quadrupled between 1971 and 1993, and by the end of the century Britons were eating twice as many chilled or frozen meals per person per year as Americans or the French.[28] The rise in domestic consumption of preprepared food of all kinds helped to make possible the much-changed role of millions of married women. So-called convenience food came to include ready-to-eat (such as cold cereals, ice-cream, and yoghurts) and ready-to-heat (such as frozen dinners of all kinds). Such food takes little time to prepare and can usually be stored. In conjunction with wider car ownership and the relentless expansion of supermarket chains, the daily walk or bicycle ride to the local butcher, baker and greengrocer was replaced by a weekly drive to the nearest supermarket. By 1997 Britons purchased 76 per cent of their food at supermarkets.[29] In shopping for food, the pleasures of service and neighbourly chat had lost out to lower prices, longer opening hours, ease of parking and one-stop efficiency. This development was not unrelated to the fact that in 1961 only 20 per cent of all married women were employed whereas by 2000 73 per cent of all married and cohabiting women aged 16 to 59 were employed.[30]

This major shift of shopping patterns had catastrophic consequences for bakers, butchers and greengrocers. By 1995 there were only 3,500 family bakeries left in Britain, 1,500 having closed in the previous five years alone. Fifty years earlier small bakeries had produced 83 per cent of British bread, but by 1995 they produced only 8 per cent. As recently as 1984 butchers' shops had sold 41 per cent of all meat in the UK, but by 1994 they sold only 22 per cent.[31] Moreover, the effect of new shopping patterns on village food shops was nothing short of calamitous. According to the Rural Development Commission, between 1991 and 1997 the number of food shops in English villages decreased from 9,000 to just under 5,000, a fall of 44 per cent in just six years.[32] As car ownership proliferated, the petrol station mini-mart became the village shop of the late twentieth century. Finally, yet another aspect of the much-changed character of British eating was dietary change. Some of the most significant changes were as shown in table 1.2.

Table 1.2 *Estimates of average food consumption of selected foods in grams per person per week, 1950–2000, Great Britain*

	1950	2000
Decreased consumption		
Butter	129	39
Sugar	287	105
Beef and veal	229	124
Mutton and lamb	154	55
Increased consumption		
Cheese	72	110
Poultry	10	253
Fruit (fresh)	408	745
Vegetables	850	1986

Sources: J. Burnet, *Plenty and Want: A Social History of Diet in England from 1815 to the Present Day* (London: Routledge, 1989), Table 49, p. 305 and *National Food Survey 2000* (London: DEFRA, SO, 2001), Tables 2.4–2.10, pp. 12–16.

That Britons came to eat so much less sugar, butter, beef, veal, mutton and lamb and so much more cheese, poultry, fruit and vegetables makes it clear why the total consumption of fat per person per week steadily declined.[33] Another change towards a more intelligent diet was a new-found preference for low-fat milk. On the other hand, the relentless rise of private car ownership resulted in millions of people getting considerably less exercise than had once been common. By 1998 Britons bicycled only 17 per cent as many miles per year as they had in 1952.[34]

Transport

The rise of the supermarket and all it entailed would have been impossible without the motorcar. It would be hard to exaggerate the impact of burgeoning car ownership on British life between 1950 and 2000. Just as television linked the private home to the wider world, so the car made distant places far more accessible than ever before. During the decades which followed the war, car ownership ceased to be the privilege of the well-off alone and instead became common to the majority of households. In 1950 there were only 1,979,000 private cars on the road in the UK but by 2000 there were 23,196,000, a twelve-fold increase. Whereas in 1951 only 14 per cent of British households had the regular use of a car, by 2000 73 per cent of households did.[35]

One result of widespread car ownership was that the supermarket became but one of a variety of retail stores, such as electrical appliance chains and furniture chains, which either developed their own out-of-town sites or else took premises in shopping malls. The rise of the out-of-town shopping mall was a development particularly characteristic of the 1980s and 1990s. Prior to the 1960s most people walked, cycled or used public transport to reach retail stores, so the most convenient place to shop was the town centre. As car ownership increased, congested town centres with their limited and expensive parking became less attractive to the motorist than out-of-town malls with their lack of traffic congestion and free car parks. In 1973 there were only 43 superstores in Britain but by 1997 there were 1,102.[36] Moreover, by 1994 Britain had 250 multi-store retail parks, some of which were enormous. The five largest such parks – Meadowhall (Sheffield), Merry Hill (Dudley), the Metro Centre (Gateshead), Brent Cross (London) and Lakeside (Thurrock) all had more than 500,000 square feet of floor space and each attracted between ten and twenty million visitors per year. Such shopping centres became so popular that they attracted visitors from considerable distances and began to replace seaside towns as day-trip destinations. Despite new government restrictions, three more enormous shopping malls, Cribbs Causeway (Bristol), Bluewater (Kent) and the Trafford Centre (near Manchester) opened in the late 1990s. Bluewater was the largest retail and leisure complex in Europe with 320 shops and 13,000 car-park spaces. Unlike other malls it featured a complex pastiche of English themes replete with an irregular roof line which its post-modern American architect, Eric Kuhne, described as 'Blenheim Palace on speed'.[37]

To a considerable extent the out-of-town malls' gain was the city-centre shops' loss. The likes of Canterbury, York, and Wells were not about to lack visitors, but a host of less-well-known market towns such as Leominster and Fakenham suffered in varying degrees as small shops closed, unable to compete with out-of-town prices and convenience for car-owners. What was eroded involved scale and identity as well as small shopkeepers' livelihoods. The centres of old market towns are compact – even cosy – as shops of all kinds intermingle with pubs, restaurants, and professional offices, between which one can stroll with pleasure. Above all, the old market towns have rich and unique historical and architectural identities, unlike out-of-town malls. In order to achieve a sufficiently high volume of sales to justify their existence in commercial terms, malls usually involve large buildings on large sites. The superstore is essentially a shed for selling. Feeble pastiches of historical motifs (neo-Georgian cupolas being a favourite) are often stuck on, but they are usually skin-deep embellishments which have little to do with the underlying buildings themselves. Stephen McClarence has aptly described Meadowhall's exterior as 'a sprawl of units with Toytown blandness assembled from a Post-Modernist DIY kit'.[38] The congenital problem with so much commercial post-modernism is that artificially-injected historical motifs look like what they are. The spirit is lost. Colour and visual jokes are not adequate substitutes for architectural authenticity. To be sure, ambiguity and camp can rise to high art, as in the Sainsbury Wing of the National Gallery, but such architectural finesse is not much sought after in designs for shopping malls.

Patterns of shopping were not the only facet of British life to be affected by the inexorable increase in car ownership. To facilitate the use of ever more vehicles the motorway network was steadily expanded, after a slow start. The first motorway in the UK, the M1, was not even partially opened until 1959 and by the mid-1960s there were still only about 370 miles of motorway, but by 2000 there were 2,138 miles.[39] The development of the motorway made long-distance travel by car much faster and in conjunction with ever-increasing car ownership motorways helped to foster a huge change in the proportion of transport provided by private vehicles. In the early 1950s public transport by road and rail was still the most common form of travel, accounting for about two-thirds of all passenger miles. Passenger travel by rail sank from 18 per cent of all distance travelled in 1952 to 5 per cent in 1995, and bus and coach journeys decreased from 42 per cent of all distance travelled in 1952 to a mere 6 per cent in 2000. In contrast, between 1952 and 2000 the distance travelled in private cars increased almost eleven-fold, and by 2000 private cars, vans and taxis were used for 85 per cent of all distance travelled. Similarly, whereas road and rail carried similar amounts of freight in the mid-1950s, by 2000 roads carried nine times as much freight as rail.[40]

By the late 1990s it had become obvious that vastly increased use of cars and trucks had far outstripped the nation's ability or desire to increase road capacity, and the argument heard with ever-increasing frequency was that building more roads only creates more traffic. Between 1982 and 1999 the number of vehicle kilometres travelled on all roads in Britain increased by 64 per cent, but motorways experienced an increase of 176 per cent.[41] Severe congestion was the inevitable result. The M25 – much used but unloved – became legendary for tailbacks. London too suffered from a glut of traffic, with the result that the average speed of vehicles in central London during the morning rush hour fell from 12.7 miles per hour in the late 1960s to 10 miles per hour by 2000.[42] North of Birmingham, the most heavily-used north-south motorway in the UK, the M6, was notorious for long delays caused by congestion.

As the number of vehicles on the road continued to grow, transport contributed to an increasing proportion of air pollution. By 1999 road transport was responsible for 69 per cent of all carbon monoxide emissions as well as 44 per cent of all nitrogen oxide emissions in the UK.[43] On warm days when the air is still, curtains of smog hang across much of southern England. It would be almost pretty if one did not know what it was. There have been no end of articles about the ill-effects of polluted air on people, animals, plants and trees, and some forms of air pollution have been reduced. Nevertheless, there remains considerable resistance to measures which would further lower air pollution by reducing use of the car. It would be simplistic to portray the ubiquitous use of the private car as a matter of individual predilection alone. Between 1974 and 2000, rail, bus and coach fares increased much faster than the rate of inflation whereas the cost of motoring increased by less than the rate of inflation.[44] Under these circumstances, any policy which sought to create a long-term shift in the public use of different modes of transport would have to address the problem of comparative cost. During the late 1990s the Blair government raised the tax on petrol in annual increments well in excess of the rate of inflation, introduced low road taxes for cars with small engines and facilitated the raising of charges for inner-city parking to unprecedented levels. Habitual use of the car was, however, so deeply built into the lives of millions of people that it remained unclear whether relatively modest measures would have much effect. Sterner measures remained unlikely as the government could not afford to be stigmatised as 'anti-car' by the motoring public.

Nevertheless, the situation had begun to change in at least one important respect. Between 1994 and 1999 the number of passenger journeys by rail had risen by 29 per cent, after having fallen steadily during the previous forty-five years.[45] It is likely that two of the factors behind this development were ever-greater road congestion (which affected buses as well as private cars) and the rapidly increasing cost of petrol. While certainly welcome on ecological grounds, greater use of passenger trains was not without adverse consequences, including serious over-crowding on commuter trains. Moreover, following three horrific crashes in which forty-three people were killed, the public became seriously concerned about the safety of the rail network, particularly as rail operators had failed to invest in the most effective safety devices on grounds of cost, and

Railtrack, which owned the tracks themselves, had clearly failed to invest in enough new track. If the rise in rail travel which occurred during the 1990s was to be the beginning of a long-term trend, massive investment in track and rolling-stock would be essential.

Thus far, changes in British life have been discussed in terms of the relationship between much-higher private incomes and housing, possessions, food, patterns of shopping and means of transport. Even the pollution caused by the glut of cars and vans was a by-product of prosperity. On the other hand, post-war prosperity did not obliterate marked variations between regions and social classes which resulted in gross inequalities. The next chapter will explore those inequalities and some of their consequences.

2

Slicing the pie

Although standards of living rose a great deal between 1950 and 2000, the benefits were not shared equally. For one thing, different regions continued to have very different standards of living; the North East with its declining heavy industries such as mining and ship-building remained considerably poorer than the prosperous South East. Wales and Northern Ireland also lagged well behind more wealthy regions. Regional disparities were reinforced by the fact that during the 1980s and 1990s income differentials between social classes widened, after having narrowed in previous decades. Moreover, the phenomenal prosperity of the post-war era was accompanied by an equally phenomenal rise in the rate of crime, and this development had a disproportionately large effect on those who lived in the poorest urban areas, particularly on so-called sink estates. Despite generally rising standards of living, the national pie was still sliced into grossly unequal portions.

Regional variations

For statistical purposes the United Kingdom is divided into twelve regions: the North East, North West, Yorkshire and the Humber, East Midlands, West Midlands, East of England, London, South East, South West, Wales, Scotland and Northern Ireland. Measurements of national averages (such as average weekly income) conceal the fact that there are major variations from region to region. In 1997–2000 average gross weekly household income was £538 in the South East but only £363 in the North East and £357 in Northern Ireland.[1]

Substantial regional differences in average household income are closely linked to social class. London has the highest proportion of people of working age in professional and managerial occupations whereas the North East has the highest proportion of unskilled and semi-skilled workers, who earn far less than professionals or managers and are far more likely to be unemployed. This is one of the reasons why in spring 2000 the South East had the lowest rate of unemployment in the UK at 3.4 per cent whereas the North East had the highest rate at 9.2 per cent.[2]

Regional variations in levels of income and unemployment are reflected in the possession of houses and cars, both of which are relatively expensive. In 1999–2000, 32 per cent of households in the East of England occupied detached houses compared with only 11 per cent in the North East. Similarly, 79 per cent of households in the East of England had cars whereas only 62 per cent in the North East had a car.[3] Other aspects of life also varied from region to region; for example, residents of the North East spent 38 per cent less on fruit per person per week than residents of the South East, which probably reflected the class structure of the North East.[4]

Nevertheless, while regional differences could be of considerable magnitude, rising standards of living had made it possible for people of all regions and social classes to own basic consumer durables. By the end of the twentieth century it had become possible to be poor and still have a telephone, a washing machine and a colour television. In 1950 this would have been out of the question.

Income distribution

When the twentieth century began, over three-quarters of the employed population of the UK was engaged in manual work. By the end of the century that proportion had declined to about one-third. Deindustrialisation had accelerated the trend; between 1964 and 2000 the proportion of employed people doing manual work fell by 26 per cent. As A. H. Halsey wrote, 'In the 1960s, 1970s, and 1980s, Britain has been moving strongly from a blue-collar to a white-collar society.'[5] The long-term rise in the standard of living of the majority of Britons had not obliterated social class, but the traditional blue-collar working class no longer constituted the majority of the British electorate. As recently as 1964, 47 per cent of that electorate consisted of manual labourers and their spouses, but by 1983 that proportion had dropped to 34 per cent.[6] Such developments had momentous implications for the Labour Party. Changes in the relative size of social classes probably accounted for at least four points of the drop in Labour support between 1964 and 1987, and the rise of New Labour was a result of political necessity.[7] In August 1996 Tony Blair said that 'a lot more people are middle class nowadays' and a few weeks later he portrayed the task of the Labour Party as being 'to allow more people to become middle class. The Labour Party did not come into being to celebrate working-class people having a lack of opportunity and poverty, but to take them out of it'.[8]

The greater prosperity of most Britons and the shrinking size of the working class probably helped to marginalise the political role of those who lost out in the competitive Britain of the 1980s and 1990s. The poor had limited political influence during the Thatcher-Major era: between 1979 and 1994–95, the average disposable real income of the population of the UK rose by 42 per cent, but the average disposable real income of the bottom 10 per cent of the population fell by 8 per cent. Moreover, incomes rose most rapidly for the top 10 per cent of the population, whose real income increased by 68 per cent.[9] This widening of income inequality followed sixty years in which income inequality had been greatly reduced.[10]

It is noteworthy that the decades which saw a growth in income inequality also saw a widening gap between mortality rates for different social classes. Between 1970–72 and 1991–93 the mortality rate for professional males in England and Wales fell by about 36 per cent whereas the mortality rate for unskilled workers rose by about 2 per cent. The result was that by 1993 unskilled workers aged 20 to 64 were almost three times as likely to die as professionals in the same age range.[11]

Low incomes also affected children's prospects for adult life. While relatively poor households could afford basic amenities such as telephones and washing machines, such households did not usually own home computers or have internet access, as table 2.1 indicates. In an ever more technological age, this marked difference in home computer ownership was hardly a boon to the prospects of children raised in low-income households.

Table 2.1 *Home computers and internet access, 2000, Great Britain (%)*

	Gross weekly household income		
	£100 or less	£250 to £300	£500 or more
Home computer	11	31	73
Home access to internet	15	22	58

Source: Living in Britain: Results from the 2000 General Household Survey (London: ONS, SO, 2001), Table 4.22, p. 47.

Poverty has many other ramifications, some of which can be quite serious. Poverty combined with long-term unemployment can result in a deeply destructive devaluation of individuals' sense of self-worth. Most people need security as well as income, and they also have a deep need for the recognised achievements, self-esteem, social status and friendships which work can provide. If work is not available, identity and status may eventually be found in alternative modes of life, some of which can be destructive to unemployed individuals and their families. For example, almost one-third of the unemployed who were interviewed by the *British Crime Survey* in 1996 said that they had used a drug in the previous year, compared with only one in ten of the employed.[12] What is not clear is the extent to which drug use led to unemployment rather than being fostered by it.

Crime and affluence

It is hardly surprising that an increasingly affluent society in which income distribution remained so uneven was affected by a major rise in the rate of crime, particularly crimes against property. Yet it is difficult to assess the relationship between affluence and crime because so many factors are involved. In the 1950s, when unemployment was still quite low, crime was thought to be primarily a product of poverty. If unsanitary slums were replaced by hygienic modern high-rise blocks and if education and social services were greatly improved, crime would decrease. Yet the next five decades saw not only an unparalleled rise in standards of living but a phenomenally rapid increase in the rate of crime. Crime began to increase long before the high unemployment of the 1970s and 1980s, but high unemployment probably exacerbated the problem. In particular, the rapid growth of the use of hard drugs by unemployed drug addicts became an important reason for more and more crimes being committed; hard drugs are expensive and addicts must find ways to raise money quickly and frequently.

In the early 1950s less than half a million offences were recorded by the police each year in England and Wales. During the next forty years recorded offences rose ten-fold to 5.6 million in 1992 before decreasing to about 5.3 million by 1999–2000.[13] It is too soon to know whether the decline represented the start of a long-term decrease or merely provided a temporary respite. Anyway, the amount by which crime rose cannot be accurately ascertained because crime statistics are notoriously unreliable. Less than half of all crimes are reported to the police. There is, moreover, reason to suspect that a greater proportion of certain types of crime was reported in the 1990s than had been reported in the 1950s. Most crimes involve property. Such crimes accounted for about 80 per cent of all offences recorded by the police in England and Wales in 1999–2000.[14] As a result of greater affluence there were by then far more valuables in homes than there had been fifty years earlier, and insurance companies had come to require that losses be reported to the police before claims for reimbursement could be lodged. For anyone who was insured there was thus a pressing incentive to report burglary to the police. The 1996 *British Crime Survey* reported that 92 per cent of those victims whose stolen or damaged property was covered by insurance and who made a claim reported the incident to the police, whereas only about one-third of those victims who were uninsured or who made no insurance claim reported the incident.[15] Another factor which may have increased the reporting of crime was the greater ease of doing so. Few homes had telephones in the 1950s but most homes had them by the late 1990s.

The endless proliferation of consumer goods combined with grossly unequal distribution of wealth may help to account for the rise in crimes against property, but affluence is less likely to account for the rise in crimes of violence, which more than quadrupled between 1960 and 2000. Those who lived on council estates and in low-income areas were twice as likely to be victims of violent crime as those who lived in more affluent areas. The reasons for the fourfold rise in violent crime remain unclear. There may be links between such crime and the widespread portrayal of violence in films and on television. It is also possible that looser family structures, less prescriptive modes of parenting and declining religious participation all helped to foster the growth of a post-modern sensibility which was conspicuously lacking in unambiguous moral imperatives. Moreover, there may have been a relationship between the growth during the 1980s and 1990s of ever-later entry to full-time employment by poorly-educated, unmarried working-class males and the fact that a disproportionate number of crimes were committed by poorly-educated, unmarried unemployed young males. In 2000, fully 7 per cent of all 18-year-old males in England and Wales were found guilty of indictable offences, by far the highest rate for any age.[16]

More broadly, part of what happened was that attitudes towards the law in general and the police in particular changed a great deal. In 1948, the American historian Henry Steele Commager, then teaching at Cambridge, wrote that the English

> are a law-abiding people. Probably no other people confess the same deep respect for the law, no other conform so instinctively to the rules and regulations of government or of any organization that has authority. They do not smoke where smoking is forbidden, or

walk on grass in defiance of signs, nor do they dabble in the black market or try to evade payments on their income tax, or get out of place in a queue. Property is safe, women and children are safe, life is safe ... the whole of society is one vast law-enforcement agency and public opinion is firmly hostile to law-breakers and rule-breakers.[17]

Similarly, the anthropologist Geoffrey Gorer wrote in *Exploring English Character* (1955) that responses to the question 'What do you think of the police?' indicated that

There is extremely little hostility to the police as an institution ... the amount and extent of enthusiastic appreciation of the police is peculiarly English and a most important component of the contemporary English character. To a great extent, the police represent an ideal model of behaviour and character.[18]

Who would write in such terms today? Of particular importance, during the 1990s the exposure of a series of appalling miscarriages of justice which resulted in innocent men serving many years in prison seriously damaged the image of the entire judicial system.

That the British public has ceased to place the police on a pedestal has been borne out by research. As reported by the 1996 *British Crime Survey*, the proportion of respondents who thought that their local police were doing a very good job fell from 43 per cent in 1982 to only 22 per cent by 1996.[19] Furthermore, only 51 per cent of respondents to the 1996 *British Social Attitudes* survey thought that the police could be trusted not to bend the rules to get a conviction 'just about always' or 'most of the time' whereas 35 per cent thought 'only some of the time' and 10 per cent thought 'almost never'.[20] In 1999–2000 there were 30,807 recorded complaints against the police in England and Wales. One or more charges were proved against 353 officers and 115 officers were dismissed or required to resign, 34 resigned or retired before proceedings against them had been completed, and 33 were permitted to resign while under suspension.[21]

Decreased respect for the police did not occur for one reason alone. It was but one instance of a much wider phenomenon, the decline of support for a variety of long-established institutions of national importance. The next four chapters will deal with that decline.

Part II

Orthodoxies in decline

3

The monarchy and the aristocracy

During the second half of the twentieth century, various institutions which had long been central to British life lost popular support. The monarchy, aristocracy, organised religion, marriage and the trade unions were all affected by changes in public opinion and private practice. The decline in the prestige and influence of these institutions was but one of the long-term developments which helped to create a more flexible and less hidebound society in which diversity flourished at the expense of some of the easy certainties of yesteryear.

It is hardly a secret that public respect for the royal family has declined. In 1964 Mass Observation asked 3,005 people about their attitudes towards royalty. Fully 60 per cent were 'entirely favourable' and another 9 per cent were 'largely favourable'.[1] In marked contrast, a 1993 Gallup Poll reported that 80 per cent of respondents thought that 'too many members of the [royal] family lead an idle jet-set kind of existence' and a 1994 Gallup Poll found that only 29 per cent of respondents felt that 'the monarchy and the royal family should stay pretty much as they are now' whereas 54 per cent thought that 'the monarchy and the royal family should continue to exist but should become more democratic and approachable, rather like the monarchy and royal family in the Netherlands' and 12 per cent believed that the monarchy should be abolished.[2] By 2000 what appeared to be a lasting change in public attitudes towards the royal family had taken place. In May 2000 an ICM poll measured Britons' support for the royal family (see table 3.1).

By the end of the twentieth century more than half of all Britons were no longer sure that their country benefited from having a royal family. Statistics aside, during the course of the 1990s it had become

Table 3.1 *'Do you think Britain would be better off or worse off without a royal family?' 1987 and 2000 (%)*

	Worse	Better	Don't know
1987	77	13	10
2000	44	27	29

Source: ICM, *Guardian*, 12 June 2000.

obvious that the royal family was no longer regarded with unalloyed admiration, and any number of televised interviews and discussion programmes explored major differences of opinion about the future of the monarchy. Such programmes would not have been aired thirty years earlier. This sea change in public opinion had not come about solely because of the highly-publicised private lives of the Prince of Wales and the Duke of York. Longer-term factors were also at work.

Since the mid-nineteenth century, the public image of the monarchy and the royal family has changed in at least two important respects. First, as David Cannadine has pointed out, royal ceremonies did not become imperial events until the last quarter of the nineteenth century. Disraeli made Queen Victoria Empress of India in 1877 and twenty years later Joseph Chamberlain invited colonial heads of state and troops to parade for the Diamond Jubilee. From then on major royal events had imperial overtones. As Cannadine commented, 'the public image of the British monarchy was fundamentally transformed in the years before the First World War, as the old ceremonial was successfully adapted in response to the changed domestic and international situation, and new ceremonial was invented and added'.[3] Probably the most important tradition to be developed in the twentieth century was the reigning monarch's Christmas broadcast to the Commonwealth, which first took place in 1932. Ceremony continued to be added or modified as in Lord Snowdon's staging for television of the investiture of the young Prince of Wales at Caernarvon Castle in 1969.

The second major change began with the deliberately-nurtured mid-twentieth-century idealisation of the royal family. For over twenty-five years, the late Queen Elizabeth (subsequently the Queen Mother) conscientiously worked to promote the image of a perfect family by authorising books of flattering photographs and adulatory biographies of family members, starting with Anne Ring's *The Story of Princess Elizabeth, Told with the Sanction of Her Parents* which was published in 1930. For more than two decades after the end of the war, television coverage of the royal family remained largely limited to public occasions. Thus, the coronation of Queen Elizabeth in June 1953 was watched by over half the population of the UK, who listened to the suitably deferential commentary of Richard Dimbleby. Not until the end of the liberated 1960s was a major departure decided upon. In 1969, Richard Cawston's unprecedented colour film, *Royal Family*, was watched by thirty-seven million Britons, being broadcast first by the BBC and reshown by ITV the following week. The film showed royal family members in a variety of activities including a barbecue in the grounds of Balmoral at which Prince Philip cooked steak with not entirely satisfactory results. Apparently innocuous in its portrayal of royalty as human beings, the film nevertheless involved a significant departure in its use of colour television, a newly-popular medium, to portray carefully selected aspects of the private life of the royal family to a mass audience. As Richard Tomlinson has pointed out, Cawston consciously blurred the distinction between the public functions and private lives of members of the royal family.[4] Thus daylight began to intrude upon magic, for Cawston's film did much to foster the evolution of the relationship between royalty and the media which led to the rise of a highly-competitive corps of professional royal watchers, a curious fraternity who eventually managed to turn the marital woes of the Prince and Princess of Wales and the Duke and Duchess of York into public entertainment. The embattled royals found themselves powerless to prevent this profoundly unwelcome intrusion. Instead, as two world-famous marriages collapsed, thus destroying the myth of a model family, several of those involved attempted to use the media to their own advantage, a process which eventually led to Jonathan Dimbleby's intimate interviews with Prince Charles which were broadcast in June 1994 as *Charles: The Private Man, the Public Role.* Such interviews and Dimbleby's 620 page book, *The Prince of Wales,* would have been unthinkable (not to mention unnecessary) thirty years earlier. It was, surely, a sign of the times that in the autumn of 1992, the Queen's *annus horribilis,* Charles wrote in a memorandum to the Queen's Private Secretary

> I believe we need a relatively narrow definition of 'private lives' and that there are many cases where things we would prefer to keep private must, nevertheless, be commented upon because they have been brought (whether we like it or not) into the public domain. Particularly where 'facts' are concerned the balance of advantage will often lie with correcting something rather than allowing it to pass unchallenged ... I do hope we can make as much use as possible of television. As the medium which carries the greatest weight of authority with the public, it should be a real asset in countering tabloid excesses.[5]

Charles' openness in the 1994 Dimbleby interviews involved, then, a calculated and strikingly modern form of response. The public was to be invited to judge him as the complex man he actually is, a development antithetical to the older values of secrecy, mystery, distance and awe which continued to protect the Queen.

As matters stood by the mid-1990s, the nation knew a great deal about Charles' character and views. It knew little about his mother's views. Yet it was at peace with his mother whereas it was uneasy with Charles as a man and as a potential king. This was hardly surprising, as the Prince did not appear to be at ease with himself. Television interviews had made familiar to everyone his frequent grimaces, his tendency to worry and his pessimism about human efforts. He also seemed to be driven by a continuing need to prove himself. Charles had laboured ceaselessly for the public good. The numerous projects which he had sponsored – including the Prince's Trust, the Prince's Youth Business Trust, Business in the

Community, the Prince of Wales' Community Ventures, the Business Leaders' Forum, and the Royal Collection Trust – had been of substantial benefit to thousands of people. Yet in the public eye his marital woes loomed larger than his conscientious efforts to serve the public good.

After the tragic death of the Princess of Wales in August 1997, the nation wept for a troubled woman whose extraordinary empathy with life's victims had touched the heart of the world. Yet as time passed and public emotion settled, it began to seem possible that Diana's death had helped to resolve a previously insoluble problem for the royal family. Within a year after her death, public sentiment towards Charles had altered greatly, and in his favour. According to MORI polls, before Diana's death only 42 per cent of the public claimed to be satisfied with the way in which Prince Charles was 'doing his job' whereas by August 1998, 63 per cent were satisfied.[6] This marked shift in public sentiment probably had little to do with how Charles carried out his royal duties and a lot to do with profound relief that a highly-publicised and seemingly endless royal controversy had finally subsided.

In discussing such matters it would be easy to overemphasise the importance of short-term swings of public opinion. Monarchy is not a popularity contest, after all. Nevertheless, it is clear that fundamental questions have arisen as to the future role of the monarchy. The Queen has been devoted to the Commonwealth of which she is the symbolic head, whereas she could hardly perform the same role within the European Union. But it is not unreasonable to wonder whether it is still appropriate to place so much royal emphasis on the former empire in Britain's increasingly post-imperial present. In recent decades the centrality of the Commonwealth to British interests has decreased, whereas links with Europe have become far more important. No one knows the future course of Britain's relations with Europe, a matter on which there are deep divisions of opinion (which will be discussed in Chapter 13), but if Britain acquires a greater sense of belonging to a European context that development will have implications for the monarchy. As

Vernon Bogdanor has written, 'The monarchy may have to develop new forms of symbolism so that the head of the nation can represent Britain as a member of the European Union. Monarchy, after all, is essentially an institution of the imagination, as Disraeli and Bagehot so well understood.'[7]

A second question concerning the future of the monarchy is that to many observers the existing royal lifestyle seems out-of-date and inappropriate. There is a sense in which the decline of the landed aristocracy has played a greater role than is sometimes realised in contributing to the growth of this impression. In the early years of the twentieth century wealthy landed aristocrats still retained exclusive possession of huge houses and retinues of servants. As long as the likes of Blenheim, Hatfield House, Chatsworth and a host of others remained closed worlds reserved for the highly privileged alone, there was not an enormous qualitative difference between the lives of the great aristocratic families and the life of the royal family itself. Ross McKibbin has written of George V that 'his tastes and style of life were those of any large hereditary English landowner' and of George VI that 'entirely surrounded by the landed classes, intimately connected to them by marriage and style of life, he found the world beyond them difficult to apprehend; there were those within the magic circle, and there were those who were not'.[8] During the second half of the twentieth century much changed. For one thing, many of the vast houses of the landed aristocracy were either given to the National Trust or else opened to the public on an unashamedly commercial basis by owners who now lived in much-reduced circumstances in wings or upper floors. No longer secure in their role, many of the dwindling band of aristocrats who still inhabited stately homes recast themselves as guardians of the nation's architectural heritage, the national interest and self-interest being construed as conveniently synonymous. The pressing need to turn great houses into commercially viable entities also brought about a proliferation of popular 'attractions' such as animal parks, miniature railways, and collections of antique cars. Indeed, in some instances – and in this Beaulieu stands out – the attractions became more noteworthy than the house itself. Between 1950 and 1965 alone about 600 houses were opened to the public, which made much use of its new-found access to previously closed houses and gardens. That access was also a boon to the immense growth of international tourism which became so vital a part of the British economy.

The diminished lifestyle of the aristocracy has helped to make the lifestyle of the royal family seem considerably more singular than it did sixty or eighty years ago. Whereas the great aristocratic houses of London have entirely disappeared, the royal family still live in palaces in which they continue to enjoy a plentiful supply of servants and a grand style of living. The entire family still depends on enormous inherited wealth not to mention inherited social position after a century in which the importance of both steadily diminished as Britain became more meritocratic, a process which has not yet run its course.

By the late 1990s change was well under way. The opening of Buckingham Palace to the public was a belated step in the direction taken many years earlier by the aristocratic owners of stately homes. The Queen's agreeing to pay income tax and to reduce the number of royal family members dependent on the civil list were also steps towards a more equitable scheme of things. Moreover, the retirement of the royal yacht *Britannia* in 1997 hardly lacked symbolic overtones. The general direction of these steps was consistent, but the nature of possible further steps was a matter for protracted discussion. In August 1996 it was reported that the most senior members of the royal family had begun to hold regular meetings of what they called The Way Forward Group, at which proposals for the future of the monarchy were discussed. Among the possibilities considered were ending the monarch's role as head of the Church of England, allowing kings and queens to marry Catholics, allowing female members of the royal family equal rights to the throne, and restricting membership of the royal family to the monarch, the consort, and children and grandchildren who are direct heirs.[9] Other possibilities were discussed after the death of the Princess of Wales.

Many of the proposals would require parliamentary approval, and a variety of potential consequences would have to be taken into account. It would be particularly important to preserve the humanitarian role played by members of the royal family as patrons of thousands of charities. Frank Prochaska, the historian of royal charity, has written that an educated estimate would be that the patronage of the extended royal family is worth at least £100 million per year to the voluntary sector.[10] A slimmed-down Dutch or Scandinavian style royal family might be in no position to continue to play this role on such a scale. Major reforms could have a variety of consequences.

4

Religion

By law the monarch is Supreme Governor of the Church of England and Defender of the Faith. If the Queen and her family had to endure the slings and arrows which culminated in her *annus horribilis*, 1992, so the church she governed also suffered from a variety of wounds, some self-inflicted but others the result of a continuing loss of members as well as loss of its once paramount position. It was hardly by chance that the Prince of Wales told Jonathan Dimbleby that 'as sovereign, he would hope to be "Defender of Faith" rather than "Defender of *the* Faith"'.[1] Charles' declaration reflected not only his own spiritual journey and deep interest in non-Christian religions but his understanding that Britain was evolving into an increasingly multi-religious society in which the most rapidly growing faiths were not Christian, let alone Anglican. By the beginning of 1999, the bishops of the Church of England were seriously considering the possibility of introducing a multi-faith ceremony for Charles' coronation.[2]

The second half of the twentieth century was not kind to the Church of England. By any number of measurements – whether of membership, attendance, confirmations, number of churches or number of clergy – Anglicanism declined precipitously. Between 1950 and 1995, adult membership fell from about 3,000,000 to 1,785,000.[3] Active participation fell even more steeply. The number of confirmations fell from 190,713 in 1960 to only 40,881 in 1997.[4] Dwindling congregations resulted in Anglican churches closing at the rate of about one a week. The number of clergy also declined. By 2000 there were only one-third as many Anglican clergy per head of population as there were in 1900. Moreover, the emoluments of Anglican clergy decreased at an alarming rate –

between 1972 and 1994 the average stipend fell by 23 per cent whereas the retail price index rose by 22 per cent. The situation was not helped by disastrous speculation in property by the Church Commissioners towards the end of the 1980s boom, which caused the church's assets to shrink from about £2.9 billion in 1989 to only £2.2 billion by 1993 before returning to their former level by the end of 1996.[5]

The Church of England had other problems as well. Liturgical flux created a feeling of impermanence which some Anglicans found deeply unsettling, and the 1980s and 1990s also saw the traumatic debate over the ordination of women, no outcome of which could possibly have satisfied all concerned. Moreover, no post-war Archbishop of Canterbury was accorded the great affection and esteem in which the late Cardinal Hume was held. It would be wrong, however, to portray such issues as major sources of the long-term decline in Anglican membership inasmuch as the other major Christian denominations experienced more or less similar declines, as did Judaism. Between 1970 and 1995 the Trinitarian churches of Britain lost about one-third of their members: Roman Catholicism lost 29 per cent, the Presbyterians lost 33 per cent, the Methodists lost 38 per cent and the Anglicans lost 40 per cent.[6] The simple fact was that most Britons no longer practised a formal religion on a regular basis. By 1999 only 12 per cent of the population attended a religious service at least once a week, and this figure included substantial attendance at non-Christian services.[7]

Loss of membership in the Trinitarian churches was accompanied by loss of political influence. In 1994, Sunday opening of retail businesses for at least six hours became legal in England and Wales despite considerable opposition from religious groups. By the late 1990s slightly over a million people still entered Church of England premises each Sunday but 1.5 million people entered their local branch of Sainsbury's, and Sunday had become Sainsbury's busiest day of the week in terms of sales per hour. Eleven million Britons now went shopping on Sunday, which was considerably more than the number who attended church, although how many did both was

anyone's guess.[8] Inability to defeat Sunday opening legislation was
but the most recent example of the churches' major loss of political
influence. Slightly over one hundred years earlier, Gladstone
refused to back Parnell in the O'Shea divorce case because as a
Liberal Prime Minister he so feared the political impact of non-con-
formist disapproval. By the end of the twentieth century Britain was
dotted with derelict chapels, and the churches as a whole no longer
spoke for a large enough segment of the population to have a deci-
sive influence on politicians. In *Faith in the City* (1985) the Anglican
Church attacked the laissez-faire policies of the Thatcher government, but to no avail. Even the devout were now apt to feel free to
pick and choose among doctrines, a phenomenon hardly confined
to Britons alone; after all, millions of Catholics now practised arti-
ficial birth control. The Pope might be respected but he was not necessarily obeyed.

By the late twentieth century, growth of active membership in
organised religions in Britain was confined to the religions practised
by Asian immigrants and their British-born sons and daughters.
Between 1970 and 1995 membership in non-Christian religions
almost tripled, rising from 450,000 to 1,300,000 members, an
increase largely made up of Muslims and Sikhs. By 1995 there were
five times as many Muslims as there had been in 1970 with the result
that Britain contained more Muslims than Methodists.[9] The substantial increase in the membership of non-Christian religions was
less a result of Asian immigration, most of which occurred before
1970, than of the high birth-rate of the relatively youthful British-
Asian population with its strong communal and family ties, its
greater disapproval of premarital sex and its strong need to confirm
personal identity and group loyalty through religious practice. In
the UK in 1994, six out of ten women of Bangladeshi/Pakistani
family origins were raising children as compared with only three out
of ten women who were not members of ethnic minorities.[10] The
burgeoning number of devout Muslims, Hindus and Sikhs in
Britain was not without controversy, but the permanent presence of
far more non-Christian citizens than ever before was certainly one

of the factors which had turned Britain into a more diverse and flexible society. A detailed analysis of the role of ethnic minorities in British life will be presented in Chapter 8.

The other large group of UK citizens for whom religion continued to play a central role were the residents of Northern Ireland. England, Scotland and Wales had become predominantly secular societies but Northern Ireland had not. While only about 12 per cent of mainland Britons attended religious services on a regular basis, well over half of the residents of Northern Ireland did so. Church attendance in the province was higher than in any western European nation other than the Republic of Ireland. Ninety per cent of the Catholics of Northern Ireland and 65 per cent of the Presbyterians (the largest Protestant denomination) were frequent or regular church attenders.[11]

For many in Northern Ireland, church attendance expressed religious belief. One survey found that 57 per cent of Northern Irish respondents 'know God exists' whereas only 10 per cent of British respondents made that claim.[12] Church attendance was also the outward and visible sign of tribal loyalty. Separate Protestant and Catholic identities were reinforced by separate schools (Protestant children attended state schools whereas Catholic children attended Catholic schools) and by separate places of residence (working-class Protestants and Catholics usually lived in separate districts). In turn, most of the political parties of Northern Ireland reflected that fractured society. All but one of those political parties represented either Protestants' or Catholics' aspirations for national identity. In 1994, 71 per cent of Northern Irish Protestants saw themselves as British (compared with only 10 per cent of Northern Irish Catholics), whereas 62 per cent of Northern Irish Catholics (but only 3 per cent of Protestants) saw themselves as Irish.[13] Most Protestants supported Unionist parties whereas most Catholics supported nationalist parties (a situation made possible by the fact that Northern Ireland does not have the same political parties as the rest of the UK). It is probably fair to say that the conflict in Northern Ireland was not so much a conflict between religions as a conflict between incompatible concepts of national identity in which religion played a central role.

At the end of the twentieth century, it remained unclear whether the long-drawn-out peace process in Northern Ireland would eventually prove to have been a watershed in the history of that troubled province. If the peace process provided a durable framework for self-rule and if close cooperation between the governments of the United Kingdom and the Republic of Ireland continued, it was possible that religion would come to play a less divisive role in Northern Irish society.

5

Marriage

One of religion's most important social functions has always been to mark and sanctify the crossing of life's great boundaries – birth, maturity, marriage and death. During the second half of the twentieth century the substantial decline in church and synagogue attendance was accompanied by decreased belief in traditional religious teachings relating to marriage, the third orthodoxy in decline which will be discussed. For most Britons, getting married became less of a transition than it once was because of widespread indifference to religious taboos against sexual intercourse and cohabitation prior to marriage. According to research carried out in 1990–91, those with no religious affiliation were the least likely to disapprove of premarital sex; only 3 per cent of men and 4 per cent of women in this group disapproved. In contrast, Christian nonconformists such as Baptists were somewhat more likely to disapprove, but those most likely to disapprove were members of non-Christian religions of whom 46 per cent of men and 41 per cent of women believed premarital sex to be wrong.[1] The negligible proportion of those with no religious affiliation who disapproved suggests that the decline of membership in organised religions was one of the factors which led to increased premarital sex. There was also a sharp decline in the acceptance of religious stigmatisation of divorce. The words 'till death us do part' had lost much of their significance now that there was one divorce for every two marriages.

The decline of religious adherence was only one of a variety of factors which brought about a decline in the relative size of the married segment of the adult population and an even greater decline in the proportion of married couples with dependent children. In 1951, 65 per cent of all men and women in England and Wales aged

15 and over were married, but by 2000 only 52 per cent of all men and women aged 16 and over were married.[2] In 1961, 38 per cent of British households consisted of couples with dependent children but by 2000 only 21 per cent of British households were of this character.[3] The interrelated factors which helped to bring about these changes included a much earlier median age at first intercourse, rising abortion, later age at first marriage, an increase in unmarried cohabitation, a greater proportion of children born outside marriage, later age at childbirth, a lower birth-rate, and a sharply rising rate of divorce. Each of these factors will be explored in turn.

As the invaluable research of Wellings, Field, Johnson and others has shown, the median age at first heterosexual intercourse has dropped considerably for both men and women. During the fifty years ending in 2000, the median age at first intercourse fell from 20 to 16 for men and from 21 to 16 for women.[4] On the other hand, between 1961 and 2000 the median age at first marriage rose by about by about four years for men and women alike, to 29.6 for men and 27.6 for women, after having fallen to unusually low levels in the previous three decades.[5] These two factors increased the average number of years between first intercourse and marriage to approximately thirteen years for men and eleven years for women. By 1990–91 only 6 per cent of men and 16 per cent of women aged 16 to 59 had experienced intercourse for the first time within marriage. Moreover, of sexually-experienced young men and women aged 16 to 24 less than 1 per cent had been married when they first had sexual intercourse.[6] Marriage was no longer a prerequisite for sex, so one reason for relatively early marriage had virtually disappeared.

Obviously changes in sexual practice would not have occurred without the combined effects of medical advances in general and more sophisticated contraception in particular. It would, however, be wrong to overemphasize the role of the pill or the oft-cited 1960s in this regard. Philip Larkin may have first experienced sexual intercourse in 1963 as 'a brilliant breaking of the bank' and believed that 'everyone felt the same' at the time, but sexual liberation actually took a lot longer.[7] Prior to the advent of AIDS, sex was gradually made safer by improved treatment of venereal disease as well as by improved methods of contraception. From salvarsan (1910) to antibiotics (after 1945) the treatment of venereal disease became far more effective; by the 1960s gonorrhoea and syphilis could both be cured within weeks. As to contraception, the pill first became available in 1961 but was not widely available for unmarried women until family planning services were brought into the National Health Service in 1974. Yet the most rapid decrease in the average age at first intercourse occurred during the 1950s, well before the advent of the pill let alone its wide availability.[8] Anyway, while the pill did become the most popular method of contraception its use was hardly universal; by 1998–99, 72 per cent of women aged 16 to 49 or their partners used some form of contraception but only 24 per cent used the pill.[9]

While the 1960s did not witness a sexual revolution as such, the liberated ethos of that decade did produce a climate of opinion particularly hospitable to social innovation. That climate made possible major legislation relating to abortion, another development which was to affect the average age at first marriage. The 1967 Abortion Act made abortion legal as long as two doctors agreed that it was necessary on medical or psychological grounds. The number of abortions for single women increased from 63,400 in 1971 to 125,024 in 1997. By 1997, 69 per cent of all abortions were performed on single women, who thus terminated pregnancies which would once have made marriage hard to avoid.[10]

Two other factors which also had a major impact on the average age at first marriage were the longer period of time spent by young women in education and the rise in the employment of women. The Robbins Report (1963) set the stage for what became a rapid expansion of educational opportunities for both sexes, but especially for women. The total number of women enrolled in higher education surged from 127,300 in 1965–66 to 1,091,800 in 1999–2000, and this increase was more than twice the increase in the total number of men enrolled.[11] Women's employment also grew, from 33 per cent of all employees in 1961 to about 44 per cent by 2000.[12] These two developments made postponement of marriage an increasingly attractive option for young women who no longer needed to marry either for sex or for maintenance and for whom early marriage and childbearing might thwart career ambitions.

In addition to fostering later marriage, women's increased earnings capacity helped to make divorce a more viable option, and by 1999 70 per cent of divorces were granted to women. Like the Abortion Act of 1967, the Divorce Act of 1969 was a product of the relatively brief 'permissive moment' of the late 1960s. The act made irretrievable breakdown of marriage the sole criterion for divorce. In 2000, 154,628 divorces were granted in the United Kingdom, more than double the number granted in 1971 when the act went into effect.[13] Divorce was also made easier by the Matrimonial and Family Proceedings Act of 1984 which allowed couples to petition for divorce after only one year of marriage whereas under previous legislation couples could not usually petition for divorce until after three years of marriage.[14] In 1971 there were only 296,000 divorced women in England and Wales, but by 2000 there were 2,063,000, a phenomenal rise.[15]

Increased divorce not only contributed to the decline of marriage but to a rapid increase in the proportion of families with dependent children headed by women. The proportion of lone parent families soared from 8 per cent in 1971 to 26 per cent by 2000–1, and 88 per cent of these parents were women.[16] In 1960 only 5 per cent of live births took place outside of marriage (a rate which had been fairly constant for most of the twentieth century), but by 2000 39 per cent of live births in England and Wales took place outside marriage. Children born to cohabiting but unmarried couples were twice as likely to end up in broken homes as children born to married couples, cohabitation being much less stable than marriage.[17] Absent fathers were not necessarily a dependable source of income, yet it remained difficult if not impossible for lone mothers to care for small children and earn a decent living at the same time. Women's wages remained lower than those of men and child-care costs could be prohibitively expensive for low paid women. In 1997 the unemployment rate for lone mothers was 16 per cent.[18] This situation produced a dilemma for the Blair government when Labour MPs were deeply upset by the prospect of a decrease in state support for single mothers and their children, even if the Prime Minister himself told the House 'we believe the most important thing is to help those lone parents off benefits and into work and do so in a way that doesn't lose control of public finances.'[19] A breakthrough came in March 1998 when Gordon Brown, the Chancellor of the Exchequer, announced that a new childcare tax credit would cover up to 70 per cent of the cost of child care for one-child families earning under £14,000 per year and for families with two or more children earning under £17,000 per year. The new tax credit was widely welcomed by those deeply concerned with the special difficulties of single mothers.

In addition to the rapid increase in the number of one-parent families there were significant changes within marriage itself. By 2000 the average age of married women at childbirth reached 29.6 years for first births.[20] Later marriage, later childbirth, and fewer children combined with ever-increasing longevity meant that a smaller proportion than ever before of the adult years of a married woman now involved bearing and caring for children. This development probably reflected not only increased ability to control fertility but the far greater value placed on obtaining a relatively high standard of living. As family size has decreased, the employment of married women has risen substantially. As has already been pointed out, in the early years of the twentieth century only about 10 per cent of all married women were employed but by 2000 73 per cent of all married and cohabiting women of working age were employed either full or part-time.[21] The balance between motherhood, education and work has shifted considerably and there is no reason to believe that development has run its course.

6

The trade unions

Trade unions have been yet another institution in decline. Since 1979, the year Margaret Thatcher became Prime Minister, there has been a major decline in the membership, power and political influence of the unions. In 1979, 53 per cent of the civilian workforce in employment belonged to unions, but by 2000 only 30 per cent of the workforce did.[1] In the wake of deindustrialisation there has also been a long-term decline in the proportion of union members who are white and male and work in heavy industry. The once strong connection between union membership and social class has blurred; an increasingly large proportion of union members are teachers, nurses, and civil servants and a correspondingly smaller proportion of union members are blue-collar workers. By 1994, UNISON, which represents workers in the public sector, had become Britain's largest union with 1.5 million members, the majority of whom were women.[2]

The origins of the decline of union membership lay partly in the character of post-war nationalisation. The Labour government elected in 1945 nationalised coal in 1946 and electricity, gas, steel and the railways in 1947, but despite the scope of these innovations nationalisation fell short of socialist ideals in that it left 80 per cent of British industry in private hands. Clause IV of the Labour party constitution, adopted in 1918, had committed the party to secure 'common ownership of the means of production'.[3] But what did this mean? Under the nationalisations of 1946 and 1947, neither the workers in nationalised industries nor the unions which represented them were given management roles or a stake in the efficiency of their own industries, let alone a controlling interest. Those industries were to be managed on behalf of the British people, but the nation's need for low cost power, heat or transport, not to mention low inflation, could be at odds with industrial workers' natural interest in secure employment, higher wages, and shorter hours. Nationalisation thus placed future Labour governments in an ambiguous and potentially untenable position in that the loyalties of any Labour government could be divided between, on the one hand, the need to control inflation and manage nationalised industries and public services in an efficient manner, and, on the other, the need to maintain long-standing and deeply-felt ties to the trade unions which had created the Labour Party and continued to be its chief source of income. By the 1970s this incipient conflict of Labour loyalties had been compounded by the increased unionisation of public-service employees.

As long as Britain was able to retain the full employment and low inflation of the 1950s and 1960s it was usually possible to form a consensus as to the possible scope of industrial settlements. Strikes, if they occurred, rarely lasted very long. In the wake of the labour unrest of the early 1970s, the oil crisis of 1973 and the serious unemployment and inflation which followed, consensus collapsed. The Heath government's ill-fated Industrial Relations Act of 1971, which depended on voluntary participation, proved to be unworkable as employers and unions failed to make collective agreements legally binding and unions boycotted the National Industrial Relations Court which the act had established. The miners' strike of 1972 in which secondary boycotts and sporadic violence were used resulted in a 20 per cent pay increase, and in 1974 another miners' strike for more pay brought down the faltering Heath government. Subsequently, under the hyperinflation of the mid-1970s, unions vied with each other in a frenzied attempt to keep up with inflation and maintain long-standing pay differentials. Other increasingly serious problems included the continued growth of the closed shop, the ease with which strikes could be approved on the basis of hands raised at mass meetings (a process which could invite intimidation), violence on picket lines, the use of flying pickets and secondary boycotts of unrelated industries. These practices were not new, but their impact increased greatly during the 1970s, which differed from the 1950s and 1960s in that strikes lasted far longer and the number of days lost to industrial disputes was far higher. During the 1950s the average number of work days lost to industrial disputes had been 3,252,900 per year and during the 1960s that figure rose slightly to 3,554,600 days per year, but during the 1970s an average of 12,870,400 work days were lost each year and the 29,474,000 work days lost in 1979 were more than twice the average per year of the 1970s as a whole.[4]

On 22 January 1979, the public service unions launched a strike to obtain a minimum wage of £60 per week for low-paid manual workers in local government and the health service. The result was that schools closed, uncollected rubbish rotted, pickets turned away the sick (including children) from hospitals, and some of the dead remained unburied. Public services tend to be monopoly providers of free or low-cost services, and if their workforce strikes then alternative services are either unavailable or too expensive for most people to use. Trapped by his own trade union past and unwilling to confront head on the crippling of those public services most heavily used by the poorer members of society, James Callaghan eventually surrendered. He later wrote,

> Even with the passage of time I find it painful to write about some of the excesses that took place. One of the most notorious was the refusal of Liverpool grave diggers to bury the dead, accounts of which appalled the country when they saw pictures of mourners being turned away from the cemetery. Such heartlessness and cold-blooded indifference to the feelings of families at moments of intense grief rightly aroused deep revulsion and did further untold harm to the cause of trade unionism that I, like many others, had been proud to defend through my life.[5]

The fault lay less with Callaghan and his government than in the profound conflict of loyalties which that government could neither avoid nor resolve.

The events of the Winter of Discontent led directly to the election of Margaret Thatcher in May 1979. The Conservative Party's election manifesto promised restrictions on picketing, government funding for postal ballots in union elections, and curtailment of the closed shop. These promises were kept, as the new government embarked on an ever-expanding programme of industrial relations legislation which was carried out in instalments throughout Margaret Thatcher's twelve years in office. The Employment Act of 1980 limited picketing to employees actually involved in a strike and stipulated that in future any closed shop agreement would require an 80 per cent majority vote of approval in a secret ballot by the workers involved. This turned out to be the first step in the virtual phasing out of the closed shop through successive pieces of legislation. Between 1980 and 1990 the number of workers in closed shops decreased by 90 per cent.[6] The 1982 Employment Act made trade union funds open to damages for unlawful actions which had been authorised by union officials, thus overturning the famous Taff Vale decision of 1901. In the event of such actions, unions could now be subject to heavy fines and their assets could be seized for contempt of court. The 1982 act also said that employers could decide which workers to reemploy after a strike, thus opening a door to the victimisation of workplace militants. The Employment Act of 1984 made secret ballots compulsory in union elections.

The miners' strike of 1984 was a desperate attempt to halt the long decline of employment in the coal industry. In March 1984, Ian MacGregor, the recently-appointed Chairman of the National Coal Board, proposed to cut coal production by four million tons and eliminate 20,000 mining jobs through natural attrition and voluntary paid redundancies. Within days a strike was called by the National Executive of the National Union of Mineworkers at the behest of the union's president Arthur Scargill, whose judgement of the situation was flawed from the start. No ballot was held to determine whether a strike would be called, an act contrary to the NUM constitution which led the Nottinghamshire miners (whose pits were modern and profitable and seemed at the time to be unlikely candidates for closure) to hold a ballot in which 70 per cent voted to reject the strike. The Nottinghamshire miners went on to set up their own union, the appropriately named Union of Democratic Mineworkers. Scargill's judgement was also flawed in that the strike started in early spring, when demand for coal supplies would inevitably begin to decrease. With existing supplies ample, coal-fired power stations easily built up stocks before the strike began.

As the strike progressed, there was considerable violence on picket lines, mass arrests, and two deaths, one that of a miner caught in a violent melee between miners and the police and the other the death of a taxi driver who happened to be carrying a non-striking miner to work and whose cab was deliberately smashed by a concrete block thrown from a motorway overpass by two striking miners. Public opinion was appalled by the violence; Gallup polls consistently indicated overwhelming public disapproval of the miners' methods. The miners also found themselves unable to evoke sympathetic strikes by workers in other industries, as they had done in 1972. Such strikes would have been illegal under the new legislation, and under that legislation the South Wales miners were heavily fined for illegal picketing and the NUM itself was fined £200,000 for conducting an illegal strike. The High Court eventually ordered that the NUM's assets be seized, a move which Arthur Scargill circumvented by sending funds abroad.

During the winter and early spring of 1985 the miners gradually returned to work, having achieved nothing. Their defeat marked an end, not a beginning. The miners' strike of 1984–85 was the last major eruption of the trade union militancy which had flourished during the 1970s under more liberal laws. It was also a major defeat for the traditional unionism of white male workers in heavy industry. The future of the union movement did not lie in such unions or in such strikes. Between 1985 and 1990 the NUM lost 80 per cent of its members as 94 out of 170 pits were closed.[7] Early in 1996 Arthur Scargill finally left the Labour Party, unable to accept the profound changes of the Blair era.

The Employment Acts of 1988, 1989, 1990 and 1993 continued the process of whittling away at trade union power. The 1988 act gave individual union members legal protection against being disciplined by their own unions for refusing to go on strike or for crossing a picket line. The 1993 act stipulated that all strike ballots had to be by post and would be subject to independent scrutiny, and that once a strike was called the employer had to receive at least seven days' notice from the union. Taken as a whole the acts introduced between 1980 and 1993 constituted a radical revision of trade union law and their net effect was to curtail unions' power and ability to attract and retain members.

Between 1979 and 1999 unions lost 40 per cent of their members because of high unemployment, the decline of highly-unionised heavy industry, the virtual abolition of the closed shop, and other measures which made it far easier for each worker to choose whether or not to belong to a union. One major development which accompanied the decline of union membership was the lessened importance of union leaders as participants in the national polity. Before 1979 Prime Ministers of both parties courted union support or at least cooperation. Mrs Thatcher, by contrast, rarely met with union leaders and during the course of the Thatcher-Major era the importance of those leaders in national affairs greatly diminished.

The power of the trade unions was curtailed not only by the series of employment acts enacted by Conservative governments but by changes in the relationship between the unions and the Labour Party. At the end of the 1980s unions still controlled five-sixths of the votes at Labour Party conferences and held eighteen out of twenty-nine seats on the party's National Executive Council. The unions also provided about 90 per cent of the party's funds. Under the block vote procedure, the votes of those members of a union who were affiliated to the Labour Party were all cast the same way. Decisions as to how block votes would be cast were made in different ways in different unions, and in some instances the decision was in the hands of a union's executive. The Labour Party's 1990 conference agreed in principle to the selection of parliamentary candidates on the basis of one-member-one-vote, and at the party's 1993 conference John Smith risked his political future by firmly backing adoption of one-member-one-vote revisions to the party's constitution. Following an impassioned speech by John Prescott, the conference agreed by the narrowest of margins that selection of parliamentary candidates would be voted on by individual members, that the block vote at party conferences would be markedly reduced, and that procedures for the election of the leader and deputy leader would be reformed.

Subsequently, under Tony Blair, the Labour Party went on to replace Clause IV of its constitution at a special conference held in April 1995. The party now sought to create 'a community in which power, wealth and opportunity are in the hands of the many not the few,' a radical but not necessarily socialist aspiration; the party no longer pledged itself to secure 'common ownership of the means of production'.[8] The change of words was generally understood to mean that the party no longer sought to nationalise major sections of the British economy. Not only had the Labour Party curtailed the ability of unions to dominate its affairs and ceased to describe itself in recognisably socialist terms, it also had no intention of repealing the bulk of the anti-trade union legislation of the Thatcher-Major era. The paralysis of 1979 would not be allowed to return.

During its first term in office, the Blair government's relationship with the unions remained controlled by budgetary restraints as well as by political considerations and it became obvious that the Prime Minister had no intention of getting rid of the trade union legislation of the Thatcher era. So-called Old Labour, which was deeply rooted in the male-dominated industrial unions which had created the Labour Party in the first place, was clearly an orthodoxy in decline. The triumph of New Labour seemed to represent a victory for social pluralism and perhaps even the end of the class war. A deliberately amorphous ideology had superseded the clear but narrow formulae of a party which had found itself in the position of no longer being able to speak for the majority of Britons.

Part III
*New opportunities,
new roles*

7

Education

During the second half of the twentieth century, education was one of the most important agents of change in British society, particularly with regard to the roles of women and members of ethnic minorities. Between 1950 and 2000 there was controversy, ferment, and innovation at all levels of education. There were a host of developments in each of the three main sectors – state primary and secondary schools, independent schools, and higher education. Each sector will be discussed in turn.

State schools

In January 1955, 1,234,174 pupils in England and Wales attended secondary modern schools, 528,455 attended grammar schools, 87,366 attended technical schools, 48,928 attended bilateral schools, and only 15,891 attended comprehensive schools.[1] Like British society, education was segmented into different cells, and those cells could determine the entire working lives of individuals who found themselves categorised at an early age. Throughout the 1950s state schools remained segmented by function, sheep and goats being created by the eleven-plus examination. The movement towards replacing specialised schools with comprehensives began in the mid-1950s. It was rooted in the work of educational psychologists, particularly those at the University of London's Institute of Education, who argued that selection lowered expectations and thus lowered the performance of children at so-called modern schools. Moreover, the English component of the eleven-plus was thought to favour children from middle-class homes who had acquired large vocabularies and grammatical skill from their parents. Between

1955 and 1960 the tiny number of pupils at comprehensives increased eight fold, and by the early 1960s the comprehensive movement was rapidly gathering strength. In 1963 Manchester City Council instructed the city's education committee to convert all secondary schools to comprehensives and abolish selection. In that same year Liverpool City Council stated that comprehensive schools afforded the greatest possible opportunities to boys and girls of all degrees of ability and that it therefore intended to establish a comprehensive system of secondary education in Liverpool.[2] Other cities soon followed and later in 1963 the Labour Party itself promised to set up a universal system of comprehensive secondary education and to abolish the eleven-plus. Leading sociologists such as A. H. Halsey strongly supported the comprehensive movement on the grounds that it would enhance social mobility and thus help to bring about a more egalitarian society.

With the strong support of Labour, the comprehensive movement flourished. By January 1975 there were 3,069 comprehensive schools with 2,459,648 pupils, far more than attended all other state schools combined. The success of the comprehensive movement brought into question the future of the direct grant grammar schools, which were self-governing institutions partly supported by state funding which made it possible for such schools to offer one-quarter of their places to children with local authority scholarships. In January 1975 only 120,944 pupils attended direct grant schools, but by being selective and including a considerable fee-paying element such schools usually enrolled many able pupils, some of whom might otherwise have played leadership roles at comprehensives.[3] In March 1975 the Wilson government announced that it planned to withdraw all financial support from direct grant schools, which could either become state-funded comprehensives or else become independent. Of the 178 direct grant schools which then existed, only sixty opted to become comprehensives. The rest, including those with the greatest academic strength and prestige, chose independence. Many fine schools such as the Perse, Abingdon School, Magdalen College School and the King Edward VI School

(Birmingham) opted for independence. Abolition of the direct grant schools might have been more of an achievement if Labour had been able to fulfil the promise made in its 1966 election manifesto to integrate all public schools within the state system. As the Wilson government failed to integrate the state and independent sectors, the net result of the abolition of direct grant schools was to create a less segmented and arguably more equitable state sector at the cost of completely separating the two sectors.

Five years later the former direct grant schools which had chosen to become independent were strengthened after the newly-elected Thatcher government established the Assisted Places Scheme. Under this scheme, state financial assistance provided on a means-tested basis made it possible for able children from financially-pressed families to attend independent schools. In removing able pupils from the state sector the new scheme was open to the same criticisms which had brought about the demise of the direct grant schools. The nature of the controversy had not changed much, but the political winds were now blowing strongly from a new direction. As Jeremy Paxman later commented, 'the ambitious middle-class saw the 1970s decision to abolish selection at eleven as an abandonment of the old grammar school standards in order to pander to the less able'.[4]

The vastly different political climate of the 1980s continued to produce legislation utterly unlike that produced by the far more liberal 1960s and 1970s. The Thatcher government intensely disliked local control if that control involved Labour councils or left-wing local education authorities, and that government's centralising tendency eventually found its educational expression in the Education Act of 1988. In January 1987, Kenneth Baker, the Secretary of State for Education, announced his intention to introduce a national curriculum for children between the ages of five and sixteen. That curriculum was subsequently portrayed as a means for producing raised and uniform standards of education in state schools; it was not applied to independent schools, which successfully fought to retain their academic freedom, nor did it apply to Scotland, which retained a relatively broad curriculum which included environmental studies, expressive arts, religious and moral education and health education. The national curriculum for England eventually came to include English, mathematics, science, technology, physical education, a modern foreign language (not required in primary schools), geography, history, art and music, the last four of which were not required after the third year of secondary schooling. The curriculum stressed the importance of pupils' acquisition of academic knowledge as opposed to skills or abilities; it emphasised traditional school subjects, not pupils' lives and expectations.[5] Oddly short of vocational options, the new curriculum appeared to be conspicuously lacking in flexibility at a time when British society was becoming more flexible in so many other ways. Simon Jenkins went so far as to suggest that the national curriculum was

> simply the traditional grammar school curriculum enforced on all secondary schools by law. There was no choice for parents, teachers, governors – or children ... the greatest irony was that a curriculum justified on economic and vocational grounds should turn out so traditional and unvocational in content. Ministers, like parents, wanted schools to teach only what they had been taught.[6]

A detailed assessment of the impact of the national curriculum would involve elaborate research which could not be undertaken for this book. It is probably too early for such an assessment anyway, given the number of years which will be required for the full impact of the national curriculum to be felt. It is, however, possible to make a few observations about educational change in the late twentieth century.

In addition to establishing the national curriculum, the 1988 Education Act made it possible for schools to opt out of local authority control and receive a grant directly from the central government. Thus what became known as grant-maintained schools were established by one of a number of measures through which local government was seriously weakened during the Thatcher-Major era. The effects of opting-out should not, however, be exaggerated. By April 1997, 1,188 out of 24,000 state schools in

England and Wales had obtained grant-maintained status, but many of those were either former grammar schools or schools afraid of being closed. Moreover, only about 5 per cent of opted-out schools introduced an element of selection; most opted-out schools remained comprehensives.[7] In 1999, opting-out was brought to an end when the Blair government fulfilled an election pledge to return the schools to Local Education Authority control, and the Assisted Places Scheme was also phased out. Broadly speaking, despite the temporary impact of the Assisted Places Scheme and, later, opting-out, the comprehensive school had continued to be by far the most common provider of state education in Britain. In 1999–2000, 85 per cent of the pupils at state secondary schools in the UK attended comprehensive schools.[8] According to an ICM poll taken in 1996, comprehensives were supported by 65 per cent of the public although 27 per cent, a sizeable minority, would have preferred a system in which some schools catered to particularly able pupils while other schools educated everyone else.[9]

Table 7.1 *Pupil–teacher ratios, 1970–71 and 1999–2000, UK*

	1970–71	1999–2000
All schools	22	18.1
Independent schools	14	9.9

Sources: Social Trends 1996, Table 3.13, p. 72 and *Education and Training Statistics for the United Kingdom* (London: DEE, SO, 2000), Table 2.8, p. 29.

Table 7.2 *Percentage of 16 to 18-year-olds in education and training, 1986–99, England (%)*

	1986	1999
Males	64	75
Females	58	76

Source: Toland, 'Change', *Social Trends 1980*, p. 32, *Social Trends 1996*, Table 3.19, p. 75; and *Social Trends 2001*, Table 3.12, p. 64.

72 New opportunities, new roles

Table 7.3 *Proportion of 16 to 18-year-olds in education, 1998 (%)*

Sweden	97
France	92
Germany	91
Belgium	89
Netherlands	88
United Kingdom	66

Source: Social Trends 2001, Table 3.13, p. 65.

The national curriculum was established to improve academic standards in state schools, but curriculum is hardly the only factor which affects academic standards. For one thing, between 1970–71 and 1999–2000 the gap between pupil-teacher ratios in state schools and independent schools remained wide. By the end of the 1990s independent schools still had far more teachers per pupil than state schools, although in both instances the ratios had improved considerably (see table 7.1).

In this respect as in many others the qualitative gap between maintained and independent education was not about to close. There were those who argued that pupil-teacher ratios were not of critical importance, but it was hard to believe that such ratios were not among the factors behind the results of the Financial Times 1998 survey of A-level performance in which 174 of the top 200 schools were independent.[10]

More encouraging, between the late 1950s and the late 1990s the proportion of young people aged 16 and over in full-time education quadrupled. By 1999 about three-quarters of all 16 to 18-year-olds were involved in full or part-time education or training. The fact that the participation of 16 to 18-year-old females had grown more rapidly than that of males augured well for women's employment (see table 7.2).

Despite these gains, the percentage of 16 to 18-year-olds in full and part-time education in the UK still lagged well behind that of most northern European nations. While the proportion of 16 to

18-year-olds in education in the UK was rising rapidly, there would have to be further rises if the UK was to have a workforce as highly educated as its continental competitors (see table 7.3).

Independent schools

In considering the independent sector it is essential to make a distinction between the phrase 'public school' and the more inclusive phrase 'independent school', which has become the commonly-accepted label for all privately-funded schools which are independent of government control. The meanings overlap, but differ in both denotation and connotation.

The phrase 'public school' has no legal or agreed definition, and its origins are unclear. The term may first have come into use centuries ago when certain local schools began to attract pupils from other regions and thus began to grow into national institutions which were public in the sense that anyone who could pay the fees could send a son. As handed down by the Victorians, the public schools were for the most part boarding schools sited somewhere south of Birmingham. Public schools were not much used by northern manufacturers, who tended to remain well outside the realms of southern gentility.[11]

The lives of pupils at most public schools were commonly defined not only by shared class assumptions but by customs peculiar to each school, customs which were nurtured and protected by the fact that pupils usually lived within their school's precincts as members of an enclosed community. The separate identities of different schools were fostered and symbolised not only by each school's architecture (quad, chapel, playing fields and so on) but by an array of idiosyncratic conventions which could include words and phrases unique to a school (and thus incomprehensible to outsiders) as well as special games and distinctive clothing. At Winchester a private language called Notions developed, and by 1900 it included about a thousand words. Still in use, Notions now includes about two hundred words, among which are 'firk' (to expel), 'quill' (a source of pleasure) and 'tother' (a preparatory school, 'particularly one's own').[12] Charterhouse too retains its own terminology such as 'banco' (prep), 'ticks' (team) and so on. Special games contributed to a school's identity and mystique, the best known probably being Eton's deliciously muddy Wall Game. Dress too denoted membership in a unique and private world. Christ's Hospital's pupils wore yellow stockings, black breeches and dark-blue full-length coats, and pupils at many other schools also wore distinctive dress. Given the wide variety of practices and attitudes which set public school life apart, it is hardly surprising that public school graduates were apt to see the world as composed of insiders and outsiders, members and non-members, a cast of mind which did much to confirm and reinforce the cellular character of the higher reaches of English life. Nor is it surprising that any number of public school values such as acceptance of social hierarchy and respect for constituted authority were essentially conservative in character. Any number of rebels were produced, including Auden, MacNeice and Orwell, but they were the exception.

It would of course be possible to write a long book about the roles played by public school graduates in British life. In 1950, 85 per cent of high court judges (and above), 76 per cent of the directors of clearing banks, 75 per cent of Church of England Assistant Bishops (and above), and 73 per cent of ambassadors were graduates of Headmasters' Conference schools as were 59 per cent of civil servants at the level of under-secretary (and above).[13] In the twentieth century Eton provided five Prime Ministers, five Chancellors of the Exchequer, five Viceroys of India, three Lord Chancellors, and ten Secretaries of State for Foreign Affairs, not to mention more than one-third of the members of the House of Lords. Graduates of independent schools have continued to occupy a remarkably disproportionate number of Commons seats when the Conservatives have been in office: 62 per cent of the Tory MPs elected in 1992 had been educated at independent schools and at the end of the Major government in 1997 18 of the 23 Cabinet ministers had been educated at independent schools, as has already been mentioned. One reason for the continuing importance of gaining a place at one of the more prestigious independent schools has been that education has become an increasingly important determinant of class. As Geoffrey Walford has written, 'In a world where stark social hierarchies have been partially replaced and legitimised by being converted into academic hierarchies, the public schools allow parents to use their cultural and financial capital to pass on their advantages to their sons, and increasingly also daughters, in a more socially acceptable way.'[14]

The nature of independent education as a whole changed a great deal between 1950 and 2000. In this regard, the 1960s were a crucible for reform. As that noteworthy decade progressed, traditional forms of hierarchy, authority and orthodoxy were increasingly questioned or satirised – the mini-skirt sent up the staid women's clothes of previous decades just as flares sent up straight-legged trousers and, by implication, men who wore them. Traditional public school mores were hardly immune to the new sensibility, including as they did antiquated and increasingly indefensible customs such as personal fagging and corporal punishment. Lindsay Anderson dramatised the collision between the new sensibility and old-fashioned public school life in his cheerfully explosive film *If*. No pre-war British film would have portrayed Anderson's fantasy school-boy revolution. The numerous changes in school life which began in the 1960s were rooted not only in the new ethos with its emphasis on freedom and individual rights but in rising standards of living. Among the changes were new patterns of authority and discipline (including changed relationships between older and younger boys as well as between boys and masters), much-improved food, heat and facilities and widespread curricular innovation.

Most of the changes which occurred after the 1960s were interrelated. Boarders, an essential ingredient of traditional public school life, became a much smaller fraction of the total number of pupils in the independent sector. Moreover, by the end of the century about one-quarter of all boarders were foreign nationals. By 1999–2000 about 618,000 children attended independent schools in the UK, about the same number as in 1970–71, but during those three decades the number of boarders had declined by about 40 per cent. By 2000, approximately 86 per cent of the pupils at independent schools in the UK were day students.[15] Forced to compete with increasingly popular independent day-schools, boarding schools had to make themselves more attractive to pupils, who had acquired considerably greater say in the choice of school than was once the case. This was one of the factors which helped to bring about many restrictions being reduced or eliminated. Relations between masters and boys became less formal, compulsory chapel was less frequent, there was more free time, older boys were no longer allowed to treat younger boys as serfs, caning disappeared, and the prefect system was de-emphasised, partly because with increasing competition for university places older boys had become more inclined to study than to spend large amounts of time in ways which might not contribute to university acceptance.

The pressing need to fill places with able pupils also contributed to an increased acceptance of girls at some previously all-male schools. Historically, public schools were as involved with the reproduction of gender roles as with the reproduction of class sensibilities. Until recent decades, boys and girls were usually educated at separate schools, and at boys' schools almost all teaching positions and positions of power were held by men whereas women cooked and nursed and did secretarial work. It would be naive to suggest that the situation changed utterly – it did not – but there was considerable progress. By 2000 there were only about 8 per cent more full-time boys than full-time girls at independent schools in England. Moreover, in January 2000 there were 19,596 men and 27,999 women employed as full-time teachers at independent schools in England.[16] In terms of numbers, women now played a substantial role as pupils and teachers in independent schools, including an increasingly significant role at many formerly all-male schools. As Graham Able, the Master of Dulwich College, remarked, 'Frankly, parents are now taking boys' and girls' education equally seriously. Sadly, twenty-five years ago that wasn't the case.'[17] On the other hand, the most prestigious independent schools (such as Eton, Winchester and Ampleforth) still admitted only boys or else admitted girls on a very limited basis. As long as this was the case women would continue to lack the special advantages which graduates of the most prestigious schools still had in acquiring high office and top positions.

Finally, one of the most significant changes at independent schools was curricular innovation. By the end of the twentieth century a far greater proportion of students at independent schools studied science and technology than was the case fifty years earlier, let alone before the war. By 2000, 45 per cent of entrants to universities from Headmasters' Conference schools were in science, engineering, technology and vocational studies.[18] Social class was largely irrelevant to such pursuits – science, while male-dominated, has never been particularly class-conscious and the ever-burgeoning world of computers, informed by west-coast American designs and sensibilities as it is, has tended to be quirky and iconoclastic. The social sciences (including business) also attracted an increasing proportion of pupils.

The growth of the importance of science, technology and social science at independent schools was directly related to the increased emphasis on university entrance and careers which resulted in a far more calculating and instrumental approach to independent education. In the age of the league table a cool parental calculus measured the standing of each school. Independent schools were seen as providing a passport to university entrance, and that perception was accurate; approximately 86 per cent of independent school post-A-level leavers went on to universities in 2000.[19] Given the increased proportion of girls in independent education and the growth of the sector as a whole, it is clear that independent schools made an important contribution to the rapid expansion of the number of women in higher education. On the other hand, the deep social and cultural divide between independent and state schools remained one of the most fundamental problems in British life, particularly as education had become one of the most important determinants of social class.

Higher education

Between 1950 and 2000 there was an extraordinarily rapid increase in the number of students in higher education around the world. Britain was no exception. During the 1920s and 1930s Britain had proportionately fewer university students than any other European country, and as recently as 1954–55 there were still only 122,000 full-time students in higher education in the UK, but by 1999–2000 there were 1,259,700, a ten-fold increase in 46 years. The number of part-time students also rose remarkably from 123,700 in 1965–66 to 764,400 by 1999–2000.[20]

These developments stemmed primarily from the enormously influential Robbins Report of 1963, although higher education had already begun to grow rapidly well before the report was published. Between 1957 and 1963 the number of full-time students in higher education in the UK had risen by almost 50 per cent.[21] By the autumn of 1961, the year the Robbins Committee was appointed, plans for seven new universities – East Anglia, Essex, Kent, Lancaster, Sussex, Warwick and York – had been approved and the first of those new universities, Sussex, had opened. Another key element fell into place when the Education Act of 1962 stated that local councils were to use funds provided by the Treasury to pay the fees and residential costs of anyone who had at least two A levels and was admitted to a university. The Robbins Committee reported in October 1963. Asked to advise on the long-term development of higher education, the committee had commissioned extensive research and had come to the conclusion that there was a vast untapped pool of ability in the UK, access to higher education being severely limited by class, gender and region. Whereas 45 per cent of the offspring of professional families entered higher education only 4 per cent of the children of skilled labourers did so. There were, moreover, almost three times as many men as women at universities, and the committee observed that the tendency for girls to gain A levels and thus qualify for entry to higher education 'may gain momentum, and this might become a major feature of the future educational scene.'[22]

The Robbins Committee recommended a massive expansion of higher education. Such expansion would be necessary in order to achieve the committee's primary goal that courses of higher education be made 'available for all those who are qualified by ability and attainment to pursue them and who wish to do so'.[23] The committee made 178 recommendations. One of them was that a Council for National Academic Awards (CNAA) should be established to grant degrees to students at non-university institutions. The main thrust of Robbins' recommendations centred, however, on the pressing need for rapid expansion of the university sector: six more new universities should be established, colleges of advanced technology should become technical universities, university status should be granted to ten existing colleges and existing universities should grow. The committee also recommended that existing university student–faculty ratios be maintained or reduced and that student–faculty ratios not be allowed to deteriorate in higher education as a whole. Universities should also become increasingly residential in nature – residential accommodation should be provided for two-thirds of the additional students who should enter higher education during the next two decades so that the proportion of students in residence would almost double, rising to 54 per cent by 1981.[24] The fact that Robbins recommended that existing student–faculty ratios be maintained while also proposing major long-term expansion of the number of university students and even more rapid expansion of residential accommodation was to have major implications for the cost per student of British universities, which were to become far more expensive to run than their less collegiate continental counterparts.

The main recommendations of the Robbins Committee were accepted by the Conservative government, which announced a

ten-year plan of expansion of higher education which would cost
£3,500 million. The CNAA was established, ten colleges of
advanced technology became universities, and teacher training colleges became colleges of education offering B.Ed. degrees.
Considerable emphasis was also placed on the residential and
architectural character of the new universities which opened
during the 1960s. Kent, Lancaster and York all had residential colleges in the Oxbridge mould and much of the more interesting
and adventurous architecture of the time was built at new universities where greenfield sites helped to make possible imaginative integration of buildings and landscape (see Chapter 11).
Architectural innovation was complemented by curricular innovation. Sussex and East Anglia both created entire schools of inter-
disciplinary studies and most of the new universities emphasised
intellectual breadth, thus reflecting the greater flexibility of mind
so characteristic of the 1960s. In the world of higher education as
a whole, new courses and fields of study began to proliferate. As
has already been pointed out, in the mid-1960s there were still
only three MBA programmes offered in all of Britain, but thirty
years later there were nearly 100.

Enrolments in higher education as a whole grew even more
quickly than Robbins proposed, but the growth of the non-university sector of higher education was so rapid that the proportion of
university students in full-time higher education declined from 69
per cent in 1957–58 to only 45 per cent by 1991.[25] The most important reason for this development was the growth of the polytechnics.
In April 1965, Anthony Crosland, Labour's Secretary of State for
Education and Science, announced the government's support for a
binary system of education which would make a clear distinction
between universities and non-university colleges of various descrip-
tions. Beyond those already approved, there were to be no more new
universities or accessions to university status for about ten years
(with the exception of the highly innovative Open University, which
opened in 1971). With no additional universities being founded, the
non-university sector began to be strengthened by the creation of

the polytechnics, the first of which was designated in 1969 and thirty of which were established by 1973. Polytechnics' status was limited by the fact that they could not award their own degrees (which were awarded by the CNAA) and unlike universities they were under local control. Yet polytechnics' costs per student were far lower than universities', partly because of less favourable student–faculty ratios, and lower costs helped to make possible the rapid expansion of the non-university sector of higher education. University costs per student were significantly higher partly because a much greater proportion of universities' academic staff work-time involved research and publication.

During the 1970s and 1980s the polytechnics rapidly grew larger and more important. The binary divide began to erode when the Education Reform Act of 1988 removed the polytechnics from local educational authority control, and the divide completely disappeared when the Further and Higher Education Act of 1992 abolished both the CNAA and the existing funding councils. Newly-created Higher Education Funding Councils would allocate funds to higher education in England, Scotland and Wales, and polytechnics and colleges of further education would not only be allowed to grant their own degrees but could become universities in their own right. The offer was eagerly accepted and by the end of 1993 all thirty-four polytechnics in England and Wales and two colleges of education had become universities.

By 1989 the government had decided that one-third of all 18-year-olds should be entering higher education by the end of the century. To achieve this end the government began to provide funds in direct relation to numbers of students and universities were forced to compete with each other to offer the lowest cost per student in each subject. The result was that between 1986 and 1994 student numbers burgeoned by 70 per cent; by 1994 one-third of all 18-year-olds were entering higher education.[26] Such an unprecedented rate of expansion created strains as well as benefits, particularly because funding rose on an absolute basis but fell on a per student basis. As the Dearing Report (1997) pointed out, the number of students in higher education doubled between 1976 and 1996 but funding per student fell by 40 per cent.[27] Academic staff were placed under considerable stress by the explosion of student numbers. The average staff-to-student ratio at British universities had stood at about 1 to 8 in 1971–72 and was still about 1 to 11 in the mid-1980s, but by 1995–96 that ratio had deteriorated to 1 to 16.6, partly as a result of the accession to the university sector of the former polytechnics. Moreover, whereas student numbers had doubled within twenty years, library space for readers had grown by only a few percent.[28] Despite such economies, the cost per student of higher education in the UK remained about 60 per cent higher than the average cost per student in Japan, Germany, Italy and France although it remained well below American and Canadian levels.[29] One reason for this was that almost half of all university students in the UK (Open University students excepted) lived in colleges, halls of residence and other university accommodation, a practice which not only had its own inherent costs but considerable implications for university-wide catering arrangements as well.

As a result of the serious stresses and strains created by rapid expansion of student numbers, on the day that the Dearing Report was issued the new Labour government announced that it planned to charge better-off families £1000 per year in tuition fees and that maintenance grants would be replaced by loans repayable over a period of up to twenty years. This announcement was hardly greeted with enthusiasm by students or their parents, but it was hard to deny that, under the circumstances, higher charges were probably inevitable. Moreover, the benefits of expansion had been substantial, the two chief beneficiaries being women and members of ethnic minorities.

Between 1965–66 and 1999–2000 the number of women in higher education in the United Kingdom had increased dramatically, and had become greater than the number of men (see table 7.4). This development was hardly confined to the UK alone. The number of women entering Australian universities had caught up

Table 7.4 *Men and women in full and part-time higher education, 1965–66 to 1999–2000, UK*

	1965–66	1999–2000
Men	310,000 (71%)	932,300 (46%)
Women	127,300 (29%)	1,091,800 (54%)

Sources: Social Trends 1971, Table 84, p. 120 and *Annual Abstract of Statistics 2001,* Table 6.8, p. 73.

with the number of men in 1979 and the number of undergraduate degrees granted to women at Canadian universities first exceeded the number granted to men in 1981.

Just as the number and proportion of women students rose sharply, so what women studied and where they studied it also changed a great deal. As Rosemary Crompton has pointed out, as recently as 1965 only 15,000 first-year full-time female undergraduates were admitted to British universities whereas 26,000 first-year full-time female students were admitted to teacher training colleges. Women had always dominated the teaching of younger children (with its maternal overtones), and at least two-thirds of the students at teacher training colleges were women. Between 1970 and 1980, however, the falling birth-rate and economic difficulties led to a massive decrease in the funds available for teacher training colleges. Undergraduate entrants to such colleges fell from 43,700 in 1970 to only 8,700 by 1980. During the same decade there was, on the other hand, a 74 per cent increase in the number of women who enrolled at universities in order to pursue a wide variety of subjects.[30]

Within the context of rapidly increasing enrolments of women at universities during the 1970s, the most radical changes occurred at the two most prestigious institutions. The women's colleges of Oxford and Cambridge had slowly acquired full status in the face of entrenched male opposition, and despite proud and distinctive traditions of their own the women's colleges remained few in number and poorly endowed. As late as the end of the 1960s, Cambridge had twenty colleges which accepted male undergraduates but only three which accepted women, with the result that only 11 per cent of all Cambridge undergraduates were women. Oxford, by contrast, had twenty-three men's colleges and five women's colleges at the end of the 1960s, and 19 per cent of Oxford undergraduates were women. During the early 1970s new mixed colleges (such as Robinson) were planned and a few men's colleges began to admit women. As the number of mixed colleges began to grow, the remaining single-sex colleges increasingly found that the academic level of their applicants was lower than that of applicants to the mixed colleges, and during the 1970s and early 1980s one after another of the all-male colleges decided to accept women. In 1984 Oriel became the last all-male Oxford college to do so, which left Magdalene College, Cambridge, to become the last all-male college at either university to accept women. The unmistakable popularity of mixed colleges had the same effect on the women's colleges, most of which opted to accept men. There being relatively few women's colleges, however, the net result of the new admissions policy was a radical change in the proportion of women undergraduates at both universities. Nowhere else in British higher education was the change in the proportion of women students so great. Nevertheless, the male–female ratios at both Oxford and Cambridge remained less favourable to women than the same ratio in higher education as a whole (see table 7.5).

Just as the proportion of women in higher education rose remarkably, so members of ethnic minorities of both sexes came to play a far more important role. Two factors make it a bit difficult to write about this subject. First, statements about ethnic minorities in Britain can mislead by failing to describe wide variations between different ethnic groups. Second, statistics regarding the admission of members of ethnic minorities to higher education were not kept by the non-university sector until 1989–90 and by the university sector until 1990–91, so it is impossible to trace the rise in minority participation in higher education through the course of several decades. It is fortunate that such statistics were fully recorded by 1990–91, just before the demise of the binary system of higher education, as the results revealed significant differences in minority

Table 7.5 *Full-time undergraduate students at Oxford and Cambridge 1968–69 to 1999–2000*

	1968–69	1999–2000
Oxford		
Men	6048 (81%)	6182 (56%)
Women	1420 (19%)	4811 (44%)
Cambridge		
Men	7371 (89%)	6146 (53.5%)
Women	900 (11%)	5349 (46.5%)

Sources: Oxford University Gazette, supplement 4, no. 3396, 4 June 1969, Table IV, p. 1241; *Oxford University Gazette*, no. 4556, 2 August 2000, Table 11b, p. 1532 and *Cambridge University Reporter*, special no. 21, vol. 130, 23 August 2000, Table 4, p. 5.

admissions to the two sectors. By 1990–91, the proportion of members of ethnic minorities admitted to institutions of higher education in relation to the size of the total ethnic minority population of the UK exceeded the proportion of whites who were admitted in relation to the size of the white population. Despite marked variations between different minority groups, members of ethnic minorities were, on average, more likely to apply for places and be admitted to higher education than whites. In a pioneering piece of research, Tariq Modood analysed the applications and admissions to higher education of members of ethnic minorities resident in the UK. Tables 7.6 and 7.7 have been drawn from his findings.

Whereas 13 per cent of all applicants to polytechnics and colleges were members of ethnic minorities, only 9 per cent of all applicants to universities were. Moreover, whereas 15 per cent of all students accepted by the non-university sector were members of ethnic minorities, only 6 per cent of students accepted by universities were. Asked why this was so, the UCCA responded that members of minorities were far more likely than whites to apply to universities in their home area, thus leading to intense competition for university places in a limited number of urban areas, particularly London, and that medicine and law were the two subjects in which it was hardest

Table 7.6 *Home admissions to polytechnics and public-sector colleges by ethnic origin, 1990–91, UK*

	Level of admissions in relation to group's share of UK population (%)
Asian–Bangladeshi	−24
Asian–Chinese	+117
Asian–Indian	+146
Asian–Pakistani	+80
Asian–Other	+140
Black–African	+212
Black–Caribbean	+53
Black–Other	−14
Total ethnic minority	+118
White	−9

Source: T. Modood, 'The Number of Ethnic Minority Students in British Higher Education: Some Grounds for Optimism', *Oxford Review of Education*, vol. 19, no. 2 (Oxford: Carfax, 1993), Table 1, p. 170.

Table 7.7 *Home admissions to universities by ethnic origin, 1990–91, UK*

	Level of admissions in relation to group's share of UK population (%)
Asian–Bangladeshi	−53
Asian–Chinese	+71
Asian–Indian	+22
Asian–Pakistani	−19
Asian–Other	+91
Black	−53
Total ethnic minority	+9
White	−3

Source: T. Modood, 'The Number of Ethnic Minority Students in British Higher Education: Some Grounds for Optimism', *Oxford Review of Education*, vol. 19, no. 2 (Oxford: Carfax, 1993), Table 2, p. 171.

to gain acceptance yet for those two fields the application rate was three times as high for minorities as for whites. More minority applicants would have been admitted to universities if they had applied for admission to different institutions and different courses. In addition, whites were somewhat more likely than non-whites to obtain A levels, and this also affected university admissions.[31]

Despite such problems, the larger picture was that the first generation of post-war immigrants from Asia and the Caribbean had arrived in Britain with limited education, had been forced to accept the most menial and low-paid jobs, and faced deep-seated racial prejudice, but by the early 1990s many of their sons and daughters had passed through the British educational system and were entering higher education, a development which was filled with implications for the role of ethnic minorities in Britain.

8

Ethnic minorities

Exploring the history of ethnic minorities in twentieth-century Britain forces one to grapple with a terminology which is far from satisfactory. It would be difficult for any serious historian to avoid making use of the ethnic statistics published in the 1991 Census, but there are problems in doing so. These problems result from practices which reflect currently-accepted linguistic conventions. The phrase 'ethnic minority' is now widely used to refer to people with tan, brown or black skin whose family origins lie in Asia, Africa and the Caribbean. Britons whose family origins happen to be European are not usually referred to as members of ethnic minorities. In keeping with this practice, the 1991 Census refers to ethnic minorities primarily in terms of country or region of origin in Asia, Africa and the Caribbean whereas it conflates all Britons with European antecedents as white. In counting members of ethnic minorities, the Census statistics also make no distinction between individuals who were born and educated in New Commonwealth countries as opposed to their sons and daughters who were born and educated in Britain, thus failing to indicate the emergence of significant educational and cultural changes between generations within most ethnic minority groups.

Skin colour is inherited but nationality and culture are mutable; for example, to refer to black Britons of Jamaican ancestry as Jamaicans would be to deny them their British birth and education and, indeed, to imply that real Britons have white skins, yet the 1991 Census categories for ethnic minorities apply the words Indian, Pakistani and Bangladeshi to all individuals whose forbears came from those countries. Part of the problem appears to lie in the lack of a clear distinction between skin colour and nationality. Thus, the

Census uses some mixed categories such as Black–Caribbean and Black–African as well as purely national categories such as Indian and Pakistani to denote members of ethnic minorities, a practice which is clearly inconsistent. The problem also lies in the indeterminate quality of ethnicity itself. As Ceri Peach has written, 'While birthplace is an unambiguous category, ethnic identity is more mercurial. Critically, ethnicity is contextual rather than absolute. One may be Welsh in England, British in Germany, European in Thailand, White in Africa ... ethnicity is a situational rather than an independent category.'[1]

Such conceptual dilemmas are not going to be solved easily or quickly, and in writing about ethnic minorities in modern Britain there is no practical alternative to using currently-accepted categories, problematic as those categories can be. The discussion which follows reflects the nature of the sources on which it has been based.

Between 1950 and 2000 there was a remarkably rapid growth of the ethnic minority population of Britain. Before the late 1940s small clusters of members of ethnic minorities lived in dockland areas of cities such as Liverpool and Cardiff, but virtually all British industrial workers were white. Many white workers were, however, either immigrants themselves or the descendents of recent immigrants. By 1851, shortly after the famine, there were 727,000 Irish immigrants in Britain and between 1880 and 1920 the Jewish population of Britain increased from about 60,000 to about 300,000, as Jews fled poverty and oppression in Eastern Europe.[2]

Most of the immigrants and refugees who came to Britain immediately before, during and after the Second World War were white. The character of post-war immigration was, however, to be profoundly influenced by two developments: The British Nationality Act of 1948 granted to citizens of Commonwealth countries the right to enter, settle and work in Britain as well as the right to bring their families. Moreover, the 1950s saw the emergence of a full-employment labour-hungry economy. Between 1951 and 2000 the number of members of ethnic minorities resident in

Britain rose from under 100,000 to 4,039,000. By 2000 ethnic minorities comprised 7.1 per cent of Britain's population.[3] There are no reliable figures for the total number of ethnic minority members in Britain in 1951, let alone figures for the number of members of specific groups. The most authoritative estimate is probably that given by Ceri Peach, who estimated the growth of major ethnic minority groups in Britain as shown in table 8.1.

Table 8.1 *Estimated size of Caribbean, Indian, Pakistani and Bangladeshi ethnic populations, 1951–2000, Great Britain*

	West Indian or Caribbean	Indian	Pakistani	Bangladeshi
1951	28,000	31,000	10,000	2,000
1971	548,000	375,000	119,000	22,000
1991	500,000	840,000	477,000	163,000
2000	529,000	984,000	675,000	257,000

Source: C. Peach, *Ethnicity in the 1991 Census*, vol. 2 (London: HMSO, 1996), Tables 4–5, pp. 8–9 and *Population Trends*, autumn 2001 (London: Office of Population Censuses and Surveys, 2001), Table 1, p. 9. Statistics for 1951–1991 are the estimates of Ceri Peach, whereas statistics for 2000 are from *Population Trends*.

Two things which these statistics make clear are the extraordinary rate of growth of the ethnic minority population and the extent to which different groups arrived at different times. Immigration occurred in waves, with the influx of immigrants from specific countries and regions swelling and receding quite separately. Most immigrants from the Caribbean arrived between 1955 and 1964 whereas immigration from India and Pakistan reached its peak between 1965 and 1974. Immigration from Bangladesh did not reach its fullest flow until 1980–84, as a result of wives rejoining husbands and new marriages being formed with partners in Bangladesh.[4]

Immigrants were drawn to Britain by the ready availability of jobs which offered much higher rates of pay than they could possibly obtain if they remained at home. In some cases, British jobs were advertised in Commonwealth countries, and London Transport even set up a recruiting office in Barbados. Far more often, information about employment and help in securing it were provided by relatives and friends who had already taken up residence in Britain. During the 1950s and 1960s many immigrants were young males, often unmarried, who intended eventually to return to their country of origin, residence in Britain being initially viewed as a money-making sojourn rather than a permanent change of abode. Many of the early Caribbean and South Asian immigrants were men from rural backgrounds with limited education and few skills who had little choice but to accept manual employment. They were by no means the poorest of the poor, because it took both initiative and some capital to get to Britain at all, but they were not well-equipped to obtain jobs which required technical skills and qualifications. Widespread racial prejudice also contributed to their having to accept types of work which whites were increasingly tending to reject, as post-war prosperity fostered upward mobility which left unfilled a residue of boring and arduous jobs. As David Mason has pointed out, such jobs often involved dirty and poorly paid work in declining industries in which cheap labour could be a substitute for capital investment or even an alternative to collapse.[5]

Migrants naturally tended to settle in areas which had both labour shortages and employers with large workforces, above all London, the industrial West Midlands, and northern textile towns such as Bradford. New arrivals naturally tended to join established communities within which assistance and accommodation could be obtained, familiar food would be readily available, and religious services would provide a focus for communal life. Roger Ballard has written of South Asians that 'the vast majority of migrants arrived not as unconnected individuals, but in cascading chains along increasingly well-worn paths of kinship and friendship ... chain migration has given Britain's South Asian settlements a far more parochial character than most outsiders are aware'.[6] The net result of such patterns of migration was that settlement became highly concentrated in a limited number of cities and regions.

It has often been claimed that Britain has become a multi-racial society, but it would be more accurate to state that Britain remains a predominantly white society which has come to include some truly multi-racial cities and metropolitan areas. By far the most important of these is Greater London, in which 28 per cent of the population were members of ethnic minorities by 2000. By 2000 Greater London contained almost half of the entire ethnic minority population of Britain, 52 per cent of which lived in the South East region as a whole. An additional 12 per cent lived in the West Midlands, particularly in and around Birmingham, so that 64 per cent of all members of ethnic minorities in Britain lived in just two English regions. In contrast, very few members of ethnic minorities lived in relatively rural counties such as Dorset, Devon and Cornwall and only 1.7 per cent of the population of Wales and 1.5 per cent of the population of Scotland were members of ethnic minorities.[7]

Between 1962 and 1991 at least three developments had profound effects on the size, role and character of various ethnic minorities in Britain. First, beginning in 1962 a lengthy series of immigration acts steadily decreased the number of migrants allowed to enter and settle. Second, the increase in levels of unemployment which took place during the 1970s and 1980s and the concomitant decrease in the number of jobs requiring unskilled manual labour had major effects on how members of ethnic minorities earned a living. Third, the markedly decreased level of immigration which resulted from tighter immigration controls became one of the factors which led to a steadily increasing proportion of members of ethnic minorities being born and educated in Britain. Each of these three developments will be discussed in turn.

Between 1962 and 1988 one immigration act after another placed ever-increasing restrictions on who could settle in Britain. Only the most important provisions of those acts will be summarised here. The Commonwealth Immigrants Act of 1962 introduced the practice of limiting the right of entry of Commonwealth citizens, who had been allowed to enter and settle without restriction since 1948; the 1962 act made it mandatory for male immigrants of working age to enter Britain with a voucher guaranteeing employment with a named employer. Subsequently, the Immigration Act of 1968 restricted the right of entry and abode in Britain to UK passport holders who had been born, adopted or naturalised in the UK or who had a parent or grandparents who had been born, adopted or naturalised in the UK. This act tended to discriminate against UK passport holders who were members of ethnic minorities from Commonwealth countries. Three years later, the 1971 Immigration Act took matters further by stating that immigrants who did not qualify for right of abode under the 1968 act would now require a work permit issued with regard to employment with a specific employer. The net effect of the series of acts passed into law between 1962 and 1971 was to bring large-scale immigration to an end. Thereafter most immigration involved family reunification and the entry of a limited number of skilled individuals with jobs already in hand. Additional impediments to immigration were added by a 1987 act which made airlines and other carriers liable for fines of up to £1,000 for each person transported to the UK who had no right of entry. Yet another act the following year stated that male immigrants from Commonwealth countries would have to demonstrate that they could maintain their families without recourse to public funds.

The 1970s and early 1980s saw the growth of unemployment and a large decrease in the number of unskilled jobs available. These developments resulted in particularly high levels of unemployment for immigrants who performed unskilled jobs in declining industries such as textiles and metal-working. Many long-established firms collapsed, and by the mid-1980s up to half of all middle-aged Asian industrial workers had lost their jobs.[8] As a result of levels of unemployment far higher than those experienced by whites, more and more British–Asians, Indians in particular, turned to self-employment. Most of them could not afford more than limited initial capital investment, so small enterprises such as sweet and newspaper shops and neighbourhood groceries were initially favoured, although some entrepreneurs eventually established far larger enterprises such as wholesale warehouses, clothing factories and food-processing plants.

In the meanwhile, an ever-increasing proportion of ethnic minority members had been born in Britain, a development which grew out of the ending of primary immigration and relatively high birth-rates among the youthful ethnic minority population.

Table 8.2 *Percentage of members of major ethnic minorities born in the UK, 2000*

Black	53
Pakistani/Bangladeshi	49
Indian	46
All ethnic minority groups	50

Source: *Living in Britain, Results from the 2000 General Household Survey*, Table 3.16, p. 23.

To be born in Britain was to be educated in Britain. Despite the gradual development of private schools under religious auspices, most members of ethnic minorities attended state schools. As has already been discussed in Chapter 7, by 1990–91 members of ethnic minorities were more likely than whites to enter higher education. On the other hand, educational achievements varied considerably from group to group. Chinese and Indians were conspicuously successful whereas Bangladeshis lagged far behind. By 1998–2000, 29 per cent of Chinese, 25 per cent of Indians and 22 per cent of whites of working age had qualifications beyond A level, but only 8 per cent of Bangladeshis did.[9]

It would of course be naive to assume that educational achievement necessarily translates into success in obtaining employment and developing careers. Partly as a result of prejudice, levels of unemployment remained much higher among many (but not all) ethnic minorities than among whites. In 2000, white unemployment was 5 per cent whereas Indian unemployment was 7 per cent, black unemployment was 15 per cent and Pakistani/ Bangladeshi unemployment was 17 per cent.[10] Obviously, different minorities were in different situations. Most young Bangladeshi males had relatively low educational achievements and more than one-third of Bangladeshi men over the age of thirty who lived in Britain did not speak English. The majority of such men performed manual labour, a particularly vulnerable occupation in view of long-established historical trends.[11] On the other hand, Indians, about half of whom were Sikhs, had been conspicuously successful in achieving educational and occupational success. By 1994–95, eighteen to twenty-seven year old Indians had become twice as likely to enter university as whites and by 1999 57 per cent of young Indians were going on to higher education. Moreover, a greater portion of Indians than whites owned their own homes and Indian households were somewhat more likely than white households to have central heating, video recorders, washing machines, computers and cars. Also, in Indian households in which the head of the household was under thirty-five, average household savings were slightly higher than in equivalent white households.[12] Sikh parents in particular actively encouraged their children to seek professional occupations, medicine, law and engineering being favoured, and British Sikhs were rapidly becoming more and more middle class. By the 1990s, the prospect of running a corner shop no longer appealed to upwardly-mobile Asian youths, and during that decade the number of small shops run by Asians declined by 23 per cent.[13]

For upwardly-mobile members of ethnic minorities, higher levels of education and career expectations were by no means the only by-products of growing up in Britain. Whereas older generations of South Asian migrants sought to insulate domestic life from what they saw as the potentially corrosive effects of British mores and tended to live largely within their own communities, their sons and daughters tended to be far more at ease in a wide variety of environments, participating in any number of educational, work and leisure activities which involved interaction with majority culture. Roger Ballard has written, 'Most of the rising generation are acutely aware of how much they differ from their parents *and* from the surrounding white majority, and as a result they are strongly

committed to ordering their own lives on their own terms.'[14] The
subtly delineated films of Hanif Kureishi gave some suggestion of
just how complicated and uncertain a process this could be.

For many British-born members of ethnic minorities, inter-generational cultural change included a marked shift of perceptions of
their family's country of origin. For the older generation, the myth
of return had the function of denying that long-term settlement in
Britain would eventually lead to cultural change. The country of
origin could be idealised as a beautiful and pleasant land to which
one's family would some day return, older and wealthier but essentially unaltered. Yet sons' and daughters' encounters with the realities of life in ancestral lands were not always easy. Between 1989 and
1994 about one-third of British-born members of minority groups
visited their parents' country of origin, and many visits to poverty-
stricken regions such as rural Bangladesh resulted in shock, disillu-
sion, and a realisation of just how much lives had been moulded by
living in Britain.[15]

Cultural distance from countries of origin was increased by linguistic change. Many British-born members of Asian ethnic minorities had limited competence in languages such as Urdu and
Punjabi.[16] In contrast, their mothers and grandmothers often spoke
little English. In 1994, 80 per cent of Bangladeshi women resident
in England aged 16 to 24 spoke English but only 27 per cent aged
25 to 44 and a mere 4 per cent aged 45 to 64 spoke English.
Similarly, 84 per cent of Pakistani women resident in England aged
16 to 24 spoke English but only 47 per cent aged 25 to 44 and 28
per cent aged 45 to 64 spoke English.[17] One of the most important
sources of inter-generational change was the growth of proficiency
in English, particularly among women.

The myth of return assumed that a high degree of cultural and
social isolation would be maintained while in Britain. In practice
the degree of isolation retained varied greatly from group to group.
While some minorities such as Bangladeshis remained largely
encapsulated, by 1991 fully 40 per cent of Black–Caribbean men
aged 16 to 34 and 20 per cent of Black-Caribbean women of that

age group were married to or cohabiting with white partners. South Asians were much less prone to form such relationships, although by 1991 7 per cent of Indian men and 4 per cent of Indian women also had white partners.[18] By their very nature such unions were antithetical to the maintenance of unalloyed ethnic identity.

A less radical but more pervasive development was that while most Asians continued to marry members of their own community, second generation Asian women were delaying marriage until a somewhat later age, a change which reflected longer periods spent in education. As recently as 1981 only 10 per cent of Bangladeshi women aged 20 to 24 were single, but by 1991 23 per cent of such women were single.[19] Increased education and later marriage both affected the employment rate of Pakistani and Bangladeshi women, which reached 25 per cent by 2000 but remained less than half that of Indian women, 61 per cent of whom were employed by 2000.[20]

Many inter-generational changes involved acceptance of some facets of the majority culture, but it would be a mistake to assume that all departures from inherited cultural patterns were steps towards assimilation. Rather than invariably accepting the practices of the majority, younger members of ethnic minorities responded to their situation in different ways. Attachment to countries of family origin tended to weaken among members of the younger generation, but in some instances decreased identification with a country of national origin was accompanied by a greater emphasis on religious identity. In minorities with a Muslim tradition quite a few members of the younger generation actively supported the religious revival of the 1980s and 1990s. About 25 per cent of Pakistanis and Bangladeshis aged between fourteen and twenty-five were attending Muslim religious services by 1993.[21] Britain's 1.2 million Muslims had many different linguistic heritages, but unlike their parents younger Muslims all spoke English and could talk to each other. Jamil Ali of *Q-News*, the weekly paper for young Muslims, commented,

Before there were two choices: assimilate or remain in a South Asian
identity ... But we in the next generation didn't feel at home in
either – either in the Western culture or in that of our parents' home-
land, which, when we visited it, was not like the utopia, the golden
land that they had described. They never spoke of the bad sides –
the corruption, the lack of hygiene. But now we have a third option.
To be a British Muslim.[22]

Whether Muslim identity will become more important than identity primarily based on countries and regions of family origin
remains to be seen. Anyway, what it means to be a British Muslim
varies from individual to individual and family to family; there is
certainly no uniformity with regard to practices such as arranged
marriage and the shunning of alcohol, let alone interpretations of
the Koran. The relationship between British Muslims and majority
culture is also far from static. Many of the practices of state schools
have been sources of dispute with regard to issues such as religious
services, the education of girls, dress, changing facilities and so on,
and it is clear that schools with considerable numbers of Muslim
students have adopted far more flexible policies than prevailed
thirty or forty years ago. Moreover, the issue of state funding of
Muslim schools was finally resolved, at least in principle, when two
Muslim primary schools, the Islamia School in Brent and Al Furqan
in Birmingham, were approved for state funding in January 1998.

Only about one-third of the members of ethnic minorities in
Britain have a Muslim heritage, and the character and role of
Britain's different ethnic minorities will continue to vary greatly.
Different minorities have reached different levels of educational and
economic achievement and are likely to face different futures.[23] In
particular, some ethnic minorities have strongly patriarchal traditions which make it very difficult for women to develop the knowledge, skills and qualifications needed to obtain employment which
is not menial and poorly paid. While some degree of inter-generational change is taking place in the lives of younger Pakistani and
Bangladeshi women, it remains to be seen to what extent they will
develop less subservient roles for themselves.

Ultimately, the evolving self-definition of members of ethnic minorities will be intertwined with the evolving self-definition of other Britons. British society is hardly static, and how minorities fare will be strongly influenced by developments which they do not control, particularly the level of unemployment. In the meanwhile, much prejudice remains. As recently as 1991, 58 per cent of Britons believed that there was a lot of prejudice against Asians and 50 per cent believed that there was a lot of prejudice against blacks.[24] Moreover, any number of anomalies still abound. In 1997 not one of the 140 judges sitting in England's three top courts was a member of an ethnic minority, only five out of 548 circuit judges were members of ethnic minorities, and only 2.3 per cent of solicitors were members of ethnic minorities.[25] In March 2001 slightly less than 3 per cent of all police officers in England and Wales were members of ethnic minorities and not one of the 46 Chief Constables was a member of an ethnic minority.[26] Finally, non-white MPs remained conspicuously absent from Conservative benches in the House of Commons. The history of ethnic minorities in Britain from 1950 to 2000 was a story of hard-won success, but much remained to be achieved.

9

Women and work

Just as the roles played by members of ethnic minorities have
become far more varied, so the roles of women have also become
far more diverse. Some important developments such as altered patterns of marriage, divorce, and education have been discussed in
previous chapters. What have not been considered in any detail are
the substantial changes in women's employment which occurred
between 1950 and 2000.

In 1951, only 31 per cent of the workforce was female, a proportion which had hardly altered since 1931 when 30 per cent was
female.[1] Women had long been taught that their primary role was
to be mothers and homemakers, and most British women saw marriage and motherhood as their main career.[2] Any number of post-
war developments were to make inroads on this philosophy. The
ending of marriage bars to employment, the creation of the Welfare
State, the growth of the service sector of the economy, the rebirth
of militant feminism, new laws, the rapid growth of the number of
women in higher education, later childbearing, smaller families,
more readily available divorce and the expectation of substantially
higher standards of living all affected women's desire and ability to
find employment and develop careers.

The marriage bar is by now barely remembered. Yet until almost
the end of the Second World War it remained impossible for a married woman to work as a teacher or civil servant because a single
woman was forced to resign from her job if she married. That the marriage bar was not dropped from teaching until 1944 and from the
Civil Service until 1946 speaks volumes for the strength of the dominant ideology of the time. As the Beveridge Report stated in 1942,
'during marriage most women will not be gainfully employed'.[3]

Whereas only 16 per cent of working women were married in 1931, by 1955 48 per cent of working women were married, a change of considerable magnitude. The demise of the marriage bar was but one of the factors behind this development. The founding of the Welfare State by the post-war Labour government led to a vast expansion of employment opportunities in the 'caring' professions – health, education and welfare – and many of these jobs were filled by women. The economic expansion of the 1950s and 1960s led to the creation of thousands of additional clerical, sales and secretarial positions which could easily be performed on a part-time basis. Such jobs were a poorly paid but realistic option for married women with children, for whom full-time employment was not a viable alternative. During the thirty years after 1951, virtually all of the rise in the proportion of British women who worked was accounted for by increased part-time employment, which was held by only 5 percent of British women in 1951 but by 27 per cent by 1981. In contrast, the proportion of women who worked full-time remained constant at about 30 per cent.[4]

Changes in the character of women's employment did not occur in a vacuum. During the 1970s, the pattern of women's work was profoundly affected by three major developments – the feminist revival, new laws, and the rapid expansion of the number of women entering higher education. It would be simplistic to portray one development as leading to another – they were all products of the ethos of the late 1960s. As those who remember the time will recall, the struggle for blacks' civil rights in the United States and student protests against the Vietnam war led directly to other movements including the Catholic civil rights marches in Northern Ireland in 1969 and the renaissance of feminism which also began towards the end of the 1960s. By 1969 there were seventy local women's liberation groups in London and in 1970 the first national Women's Liberation Workshop was held in Oxford and attended by 600 delegates.

The women's movement voiced both central themes and specific demands: The importance of each woman's right to self-determination was the theme which underlay demands for an end to discrimination in education, equal employment opportunities and equal pay for equal work. The 1970s saw legislation which promoted those aims. The Equal Pay Act of 1970 established the principle of equal pay for equal work, although compliance with the act remained voluntary until 1975 and not until 1983 was it amended to take into account 'work of comparable value'. The Sex Discrimination Act of 1975 made it illegal for an employer to treat a member of one sex less favourably than a member of the other. The 1975 Employment Protection Act made it illegal to dismiss women because they were pregnant and gave women a right to maternity pay and the right to return to their jobs in due course. These three acts did a great deal to help women obtain and retain employment, but family life in general and the needs of young children in particular continued to make it difficult for married women to pursue long-term careers which led to well-paid high-status jobs. Career breaks were possible, but women who interrupted their careers to raise children and later returned to work were apt to find that their job-status did not catch up with its pre-break level.[5] This dilemma has not been solved, and may be one of the reasons why the popularity of marriage has declined.

From the 1970s on, anti-discrimination legislation and greater educational achievement helped to raise the level of women's employment. The employment rate of women of working age in the UK rose from 47 per cent in 1959 to 70 per cent by 2000. On the other hand, women constituted only 33 per cent of all full-time employees as opposed to 81 per cent of all part-time employees and a wide gap opened up between the educational qualifications and pay levels of women with full-time jobs as opposed to those of women with part-time jobs.[6] By the 1990s, women with full-time jobs were just as likely to have degrees as their male colleagues, and by 1998 only 3 per cent of women with degrees were involuntarily unemployed.[7] Moreover, whereas the average hourly earnings of women with full-time jobs had been only 65 per cent of comparable male earnings in 1970, they had risen to 82 per cent of male earnings by 2000. In contrast, the level of educational achievement of women with part-time jobs rose far more slowly and by 2000 the average hourly pay of women with part-time jobs was still only 61 per cent of that of men with full-time jobs.[8]

Part of the problem was the lack of equal benefits and protections accorded to part-time workers by law. Employers had lower National Insurance costs for part-time workers as well as lower levels of legal and customary obligation regarding sickness and holiday pay. The low compensation of part-time women workers resulted primarily, however, from the nature of the work they did. In spring 2000, 22 per cent of all women who worked part-time performed personal services such as hairdressing, 21 per cent held clerical or secretarial positions, and 19 per cent were in sales.[9] As long as women's part-time work primarily consisted of low-skilled jobs it was unlikely that more than limited progress would be made with regard to levels of pay.

While most part-time jobs held by women had low pay and low status, at the other end of the scale a steadily increasing proportion of those qualifying for professional occupations were women. In 1961 only 3.5 per cent of solicitors were women, but by 1997 33 per cent of the practising solicitors in England and Wales were women, and there were more female than male solicitors aged thirty and under.[10] By the end of the 1990s about half of all entrants to medical school were women. The number of women M.P.s remained very low until the end of the 1970s, but their numbers then expanded, rising from 19 women MPs in 1979 to 121 in August 1998 before falling to 106 as a result of the election held in June 2001.[11] In 1961 only 3 per cent of the members of the police were women but by 2000 there were 20,155 female police officers who made up about 17 per cent of the force.[12]

As to women reaching the most senior positions, it is easy to point to a handful of top jobs which were or are held by women. The posts of Prime Minister, Director of Public Prosecutions, and Director of MI5 are the most obvious examples. On the other hand, the first female chief executive of a FTSE 100 company was not appointed until 1996 (when Marjorie Scardino was named head of

Pearson), and it remained extremely rare for women to head large businesses (the cosmetics industry excepted). Moreover, few women served as company directors. By 2000 only about 2 per cent of the executive directors of the 100 largest UK firms were women, and nine out of ten of those companies had no female executive directors.[13] Moreover, in 1998 only 7 per cent of all High Court judges in England and Wales were women.[14] Top positions are usually reached after years of hard work and promotion, and it remains to be seen whether the burgeoning number of women obtaining degrees and qualifications will eventually lead to a substantially greater number of women occupying the most senior positions in government, business and the professions.

10

Youth and age

One of the most consistent themes of this book has been the decline of support for various institutions as well as the decline of acceptance of once commonly expected forms of behaviour, gender roles in particular. Throughout human life, behaviour is profoundly influenced by shared assumptions about the nature of the lifecycle; from childhood to old age, phases of life are defined and interpreted in a variety of ways from one society to another as well as from one historical era to another. Youth and age are therefore terms whose meaning depends on both social and historical context. (Who is young? Who is old? When does youth end? When does old age begin?) After briefly discussing questions of definition, this chapter will argue that during the second half of the twentieth century the nature of both youth and age in Britain changed considerably. Youth and age both became longer and more distinctive phases of Britons' lives, phases in which formerly-accepted modes of behaviour were called into question or discarded altogether.

Youth

Youth can be defined as the period of life between childhood and maturity. It is, however, not easy to define either the beginning or the end of youth with much precision. Youth can be defined in chronological terms, such as the years from 12 to 21. The law does just that, by stipulating that certain events may not take place until an appropriate age (and, thus, degree of maturity) has been reached. Britons cannot hold a part-time job until they are 13, cannot leave school until 16, cannot drive until they are 17, and so on. Yet the legal timetables for such events have changed with the times. Thus, the school-leaving age was raised repeatedly during the twentieth century whereas the legal age of majority was reduced from 21 to 18 in 1969. These and other historical changes make defining youth in terms of age alone of somewhat limited value.

Alternative definitions of youth are based not on age but on events. Sociologists define youth as the period of transition from a family of origin in which a child is dependent on parents to the eventual forming of a family (or household) of destination. Youth thus refers to the long march from dependence to independence, the central experience of growing up being the experience of gradually becoming less reliant on parents. Youth comes to a close not only with the forming of a separate household but with the transition from full-time education to employment.[1]

It is clear that during the second half of the twentieth century youth became a longer and more distinctive but less predictable period of Britons' lives. This was true of at least three different areas, sex, education, and work. In sexual terms, youth now begins earlier than it once did. For one thing, puberty now occurs at about 12 whereas until the mid-nineteenth century it occurred at 15 or 16.[2] Moreover, as has already been discussed, between 1950 and 2000 the median age at first intercourse fell from 20 to 16 for men and from 21 to 16 for women, yet the average age at first marriage rose by about 4 years for both sexes (following a lengthy fall during the earlier decades of the twentieth century).[3] In addition, the incidence of marriage has been in decline. Thus, as far as sex and marriage are concerned, youth begins earlier but lasts longer than it once did. This picture is, however, simplistic in that it does not take into account the large number of couples who set up households without being married.

The increased length of the transition from childhood to adulthood has also been brought about by changed patterns of education and employment. The transition to full-time employment (assuming that such employment is available) cannot take place until full-time education has been completed. It is therefore of considerable importance that education now lasts much longer than ever before.

It lasts longer partly because the school leaving age has been raised repeatedly (from 10 in 1880 to 11 in 1894 to 12 in 1902 to 14 in 1918 to 15 in 1947 to 16 in 1972), and partly because in recent decades a rapidly increasing proportion of the population has decided to pursue higher education. As recently as the spring of 1984 only 8 per cent of all 18 to 24-year-olds were in full-time education, but by spring 1998 28 per cent were.[4] This development occurred for a number of reasons, including not only greatly increased numbers of university places being made available and major changes in the aspirations of both women and ethnic minorities as well as the steadily increasing importance of higher education as a qualification for employment. Ever longer periods spent in education also resulted from the increased difficulty in finding jobs experienced by those leaving school at the age of 16 or 17. Far more work now requires specialised skills and knowledge, and less and less unskilled work is available. Technology pervades our lives and technology requires lengthy training.

Under these circumstances, entry to full-time work has been taking place not only at a later age but via an increasingly diverse variety of routes. In the 1960s, most British working-class males left school at 16 and immediately took up full-time, low-skilled work. In more recent decades, the decline of heavy industry has led to lower demand for unskilled workers, including unskilled 16 and 17-year-olds. As recently as 1976, 53 per cent of all young people entered full-time employment at the age of 16, but by the early 1990s only 10 per cent of all 16-year-olds were leaving school to enter full-time employment. For an increasingly large proportion of those in their late teens, additional education or training had become not an option but a necessity. As has already been pointed out, by 1999 75 per cent of young people aged 16 to 18 were in education and training, and between 1984 and 1999 the proportion of the working-age population with no qualifications more than halved.[5]

These developments have prolonged the length of time that young people remain financially dependent on their parents. This tends to be less of a problem for youths from middle-class homes (whose families expect them to remain in education long enough to obtain qualifications for 'suitable' careers) than for working-class youths, males in particular, who have been seriously affected by the decline in the availability of unskilled work. In the winter of 1999–2000, 17 per cent of all economically active young men aged 16 to 19 were unemployed. At any one time about 285,000 young people aged 16 to 25 are on youth training schemes in England and Wales but these schemes do not necessarily lead to satisfactory long-term employment.[6] For a variety of reasons, then, the transition from school to work has become slower and more problematic than it once was, a development which has prolonged youth partly because it has helped to foster the tendency to postpone marrying and having children.[7]

As youth has grown longer its character has changed. During the 1950s and 1960s, greater affluence, increased sexual freedom and greater leisure time all helped to make possible the emergence of distinctive youth subcultures, not only in Britain but throughout much of the western world. Rising standards of living and greater freedom made it possible to experiment with clothing, language and styles of life which contrasted with those of the adult world and were intended to do so.

After the austerity of the late 1940s came to an end, the spending power of British youth began to increase. In 1959, Mark Abrams, a market researcher, published *The Teenage Consumer*, a pioneering study of the spending habits of British teenagers. Abrams rather oddly defined teenagers as those who had reached 15 but were still under 25 and were unmarried.[8] This group had become 'newly enfranchised, in an economic sense'.[9] By 1958, teenagers (as defined by Abrams) were earning about £1,480 million per year, roughly 8.5 per cent of all personal income in Great Britain. Their real earnings had increased by 50 per cent since 1938, double the increase for adults as a whole.[10] Moreover, unmarried 15 to 24-year-olds had developed unique patterns of consumption. By 1957, they were responsible for 44 per cent of all spending on records and record players, 26 per cent of all cinema admissions, 24 per cent of cosmetics, 19 per cent of footwear, and 16 per cent of women's clothing, even though their spending as a whole was only 6 per cent of all consumer spending.[11] (Part of the explanation for this discrepancy was that for many youths who still lived at home, expenditure on rent, light, heat and food was either below market value or nonexistent, depending on the family and its circumstances.)

Abrams' focus on the young consumer accurately defined a critical aspect of what was to become the new youth culture. One of the hallmarks of that culture was to be an emphasis on the importance of possessions, which came to be outward and visible signs of youth's new sense of its own special identity. To a remarkable extent, who you were came to be defined by what you owned and how you looked; appearance became a critical element of lifestyle. The teddy boys of the mid-1950s parodied the sartorial past in order to establish their own identity. There never were many teddy boys (or mods or rockers, for that matter), but as highly-publicised rule-breakers they led the way towards what was to become, by the mid-1960s, a genuine stylistic revolution. By the late 1960s it had become almost obligatory for young males to have long hair in order to signal conformity to the prevailing mode of nonconformity. The long hair and colourful clothing of 1960s and 1970s youth involved a calculated rejection of the conservative hair styles, coats, ties and dresses of the white-collar workplace, which was seen as an exclusively adult domain. The two domains could not, however, remain truly independent of each other, because youth culture increasingly came to be manipulated for commercial gain by knowing adults. Most possessions must be manufactured, after all, and not many 18-year-olds own factories. The youth market was a niche market, but it became an enormous niche market which brought financial gain to any number of adults, who thus acquired a vested interest in youth's maintaining a distinctive identity symbolised by appropriate gear. By the 1970s the hip entrepreneur had become a familiar if often ephemeral figure, although the extraordinary Richard Branson was among those who proved to have real staying power.

If distinctive possessions and personal appearance were one side of youth culture, the other side involved the exploration of new ways of living. The urge to experiment included not only taking advantage of much-increased sexual freedom but, for many, the urge to experiment with drugs. By the late 1960s cannabis (smoked by millions) and LSD (harder to come by and never widely used in Britain) marked the two poles of drug experimentation. For millions of teenagers, cannabis provided escape and release from responsibility by fostering a relaxed, disengaged, dream-like state of mind which was apt to be antithetical to the duller forms of worldly achievement, music and painting being arguable exceptions. Pop culture based on harder drugs became more firmly established in the United States (San Francisco in particular) than it was in the UK, which has no equivalent of California. No British band ever approached the haunting beauty or melodic originality of the Jefferson Airplane at their druggy best. The Rolling Stones remained conventional in their unconventionality, their musical style being essentially honkytonk with amps. Ultimately the Stones were (and remain) highly-skilled imitators, down to their frequent Americanisms. 'I can't get no satisfaction' is, after all, purely American in syntax, and the Stones wisely allowed the house called 'The Rising Sun' to remain 'down in New Orleans' where it belonged; it could not have been transposed to less exotic locales such as, say, Manchester or Leeds. Simulated as it increasingly became, the Stones' perpetual adolescence was a perennial marketing success.

In contrast, the Beatles remained identifiably British in their homey good cheer and gentle nostalgia. No American group could possibly have sung about fish finger pie, nor would an American ever have composed 'Eleanor Rigby'. As George Melly wrote in 1969, 'the Beatles have seldom betrayed their own memory bank'.[12] The Beatles remained an exception, however; less original pop groups (which is to say most other pop groups) continued to draw on

American models, just as they had always done. Back in the mid-
1950s Lonnie Donegan had sung blues taken directly from
Leadbelly (the black American blues singer Huddie Ledbetter who
died in 1949), and in 1956 Donegan's version of 'Rock Island Line'
reached number one in the British charts. It seems unlikely that
many of Donegan's British fans knew that there actually was a Rock
Island line, let alone where it ran. Leadbelly had, after all, been
singing about his own life. As the British rock scene developed, the
underlying problem of inauthenticity did not completely disappear,
and when at the end of the 1960s George Melly wryly referred to
the early Stones as 'blues shouters from the Thames Valley cotton
fields' he voiced a home truth which would have been hard to
refute.[13]

Music aside, the new freedom to develop alternative lifestyles
had other results of lasting consequence. Of particular importance,
the increased acceptance of sex without marriage provided a context which made possible fundamental changes in the legal and
social standing of homosexuals. As Jeffrey Weeks has written of the
'new hedonism' of the 1960s, 'if sexual pleasure was a desirable
goal, how could homosexuals be excluded?'[14] Why was being an
active homosexual illegal and why were hundreds of men prosecuted each year for homosexual offences?[15] As in so many other
areas of life, the developments which came to fruition in the 1960s
actually began in the 1950s. In 1954 a Home Office Departmental
Inquiry was set up under the chairmanship of Sir John Wolfenden,
the Vice-Chancellor of Reading University. The resulting Report of
the Wolfenden Committee (1957) argued that consensual homosexual behaviour between adults should be made legal, and that
those under twenty-one should only be prosecuted with the per-
mission of the Attorney-General or the Director of Public
Prosecutions. Ten years later the Sexual Offences Act of 1967
decriminalised male homosexual acts conducted by adults over 21
in private in England and Wales. Prejudice against homosexuals did
not, however, suddenly disappear. In 1975, a survey of 1,930 adults
conducted by the National Opinion Poll for *Gay News* found that

only 40 per cent of respondents agreed that homosexuals should be able to live together openly and 48 per cent of respondents believed that 'there are certain occupations that homosexuals should never be allowed to have like being teachers or doctors'.[16] Subsequently, the AIDS panic of the late 1980s seriously damaged the public image of homosexuals, quite simply because most Britons with AIDS were homosexuals.[17] By 1987 fully 74 per cent of respondents to a *British Social Attitudes* survey believed that homosexual relationships were 'always or mostly wrong'.[18] Moreover, 50 per cent of respondents said that it was not acceptable for homosexuals to teach at school, and 44 per cent said that it was not acceptable for homosexuals to teach at universities.[19]

During the course of the 1990s the AIDS hysteria gradually subsided, partly as a result of public education (in which the late Princess of Wales played a valiant role) and partly due to gains in medical treatment. Television portrayal of gay men and lesbians became more frequent, although it is debatable whether camp comedians such as Julian Clary did fellow-homosexuals much of a service by enacting the gay equivalent of the stage Irishman. In a more straight-laced milieu, there was a growing trend for political figures, in particular Labour MPs such as the highly-regarded Cabinet Member Chris Smith, to be open about their homosexuality. It would be naive to suggest that a complete change in popular attitudes occurred, but by the late 1990s there was certainly much less overt hostility towards homosexuals in Britain than there had been fifty years earlier.[20] Moreover, just as youth culture provided an enormously profitable niche market, so a commercialisation of homosexual lifestyles occurred, as cafes, clubs, bars and shops, particularly in Soho, were designed to appeal to a gay clientele. Legal change, greater tolerance and a higher standard of living had made possible the development of products and social venues designed to appeal to homosexuals. Yet for the most part, Soho and its smaller analogues elsewhere remained places to go, not places to live, and Britain showed no sign of developing large gay residential areas like the Castro district in San Francisco or Greenwich Village in New

York.[21] Moreover, the size and number of commercial enterprises with a homosexual orientation was limited by the fact that only about 2.6 per cent of British men and women were practising homosexuals.[22]

Returning to the topic of youth, by the mid-1980s those who had been young during the 1960s were approaching middle age, and the phrase 'Thatcher's children' was coined to refer to a new generation whose members were supposedly materialistic and self-centred. This stereotype exaggerated, but in considering careers the new generation did place a higher value on the importance of good starting pay and promotion opportunities than the youth of the 1960s had done.[23] Moreover, by the 1980s the youthful radicalism of the 1960s had virtually disappeared and political apathy had become the norm. By the end of the twentieth century most British teenagers had little interest in politics (see table 10.1).

Table 10.1 *Teenage interest in politics, 1998, Great Britain (%)*

A great deal/quite a lot	10
Some	24
Not very much	32
Not at all	34

Source: A. Park, 'Young People and Political Apathy' in *British Social Attitudes 16th Report*, 1999–2000 (Aldershot: Dartmouth, 1999), p. 24.

Just as youth was no longer interested in politics, so youthful clothing no longer challenged adult assumptions. By the 1990s youthful styles were largely determined by stores such as Next and The Gap and by manufacturers such as Nike and Adidas. Trainers hardly constituted a threat to the status quo. Much sportswear was manufactured in third world countries under sweat-shop conditions, but this rarely concerned those who enjoyed clothing which was comfortable and casual.

All in all, as far as the young were concerned, the most important developments of the 1980s and 1990s had little to do with either politics or fashion and a great deal to do with education, a topic which has already been discussed in considerable detail. By the end of the twentieth century young women and members of ethnic minorities were achieving unprecedented success in higher education, and anyone who visited a major British university in the 1950s and revisited that university in 2000 might have noticed how much the faces had changed.

Age

In historical terms, changes in the social construction of youth have been mirrored by changes in the social construction of age. Both childhood and old age have been cordoned off from the rest of life. By the end of the nineteenth century, childhood had been separated from both adulthood and the world of work by laws which forbade child labour and required school attendance until a specific age. Similarly, old age was made separate from the working years by the inauguration of mandatory retirement and by the introduction of state pensions. The Old Age Pension Act of 1908 initially made state pensions available only to those over 70 on a means-tested basis, but by the late 1960s the normal age of retirement from full-time work had dropped to 65 for men and 60 for women. Thus, over a period of one hundred years there had been a truly remarkable change: in 1881 fully 73 per cent of all British men over the age of 65 had some form of paid work but by 1980 only 13 per cent of British men over 65 had paid work.[24]

Just as youth was prolonged by lengthier education and by later entry to the workforce, so age was prolonged by longer lifespans as well as by earlier retirement. During the course of the twentieth century the proportion of Britons aged 65 and over tripled, rising from 5 per cent in 1901 to 16 per cent by 2000. Moreover, between 1951 and 2000 alone the number of Britons aged 65 and over rose by about 70 per cent to 9.3 million people.[25] Yet the average age at retirement fell rapidly; the proportion of Britons aged between 60 and 64 who were still at work decreased from 80 per cent in 1973 to about 50 per cent in 1997.[26] The trend towards earlier retirement was not peculiar to the UK – it occurred in all western societies. For example, between 1960 and 1985 the median age at retirement for males in West Germany dropped from 65 to 60.[27] One of the reasons for this trend was that older men were much more likely than younger men or women to be employed in declining industries. In such industries, early retirement was one way in which employers controlled wage costs and numbers of employees. Moreover, occupational pensions and invalidity benefits were both used as vehicles for early retirement by British firms anxious to rid themselves of 'surplus' labour.[28]

As the number of years between retirement and death increased, two separate issues emerged – the social cost of increased longevity and the unclear role of rapidly growing numbers of older citizens. As far as social costs were concerned, one result of later entry to the workforce combined with earlier exit from the workforce was a dramatic decrease in the number of years actually spent in work. This decrease had dire implications for the dependency ratio, i.e. the ratio between those who work and pay taxes on their earnings as opposed to the young and the old who pay lower taxes but receive more expensive benefits in the form of education on the one hand and health and social services on the other. The resulting financial strain was intensified by a disproportionate rise in the relative numbers of the very elderly, who are particularly likely to need medical care and social support. The proportion of Britons aged 75 and over was only 4 per cent in 1961 but reached 7 per cent by 2000.[29] Moreover, between 1961 and 2000 the number of Britons aged 85 and over trebled; in 1961 there were only about 350,000 Britons aged 85 and over but by 2000 there were 1,162,000.[30]

There has been deep concern in the medical and caring professions at the continuing increase in the proportion of 80 and 90 year olds, many of whom are very frail and in need of a great deal of care. Alzheimer's disease and other varieties of senile dementia have become particularly problematic as people live longer. According to a reliable estimate, dementia afflicts 20 per cent of those over 85. Moreover, the very elderly see their GPs more often, have more

home visits from doctors and district nurses, and are the most likely
to need home-help services and meals-on-wheels, all of which are
labour-intensive forms of assistance. In England in 1997 only about
3 per cent of those aged 65 to 74 received home care from a local
authority whereas such care was received by about 36 per cent of
those aged 85 and over. Between 1981 and 1998 the total cost in
real terms of social security expenditure to benefit the elderly of
Great Britain rose by over 40 per cent.[31]

The financial implications of the changing dependency ratio
pose a serious long-term challenge. Nevertheless, it would be
unthinkable to consider old age solely in such terms. It is true that
older citizens tend to need more medical and social services, but it
is also true that more people in their sixties and early seventies now
remain in reasonably good health than ever before. In recent years,
many gerontologists have stressed the importance of making a clear
distinction between the lengthy phase of fairly healthy life which
usually follows retirement and the later phase of frailty, illness and
decline. The phrases 'third age' and 'fourth age' were coined to
denote what have been seen as the two very different segments of
old age. The *Final Report* of the Carnegie Inquiry into the third age
(1993) defined the third age as 'the period of life when people
emerge from the imperative of earning a living and/or bringing up
children and, without precedent in our society, are able to look forward to perhaps twenty or more years of healthy life'.[32] In contrast,
the phrase fourth age was coined to refer to the later years of life so
often characterised by increasing disability and dependency. It
would be hard to deny that there is quite a difference between the
health and abilities of most people in their sixties as opposed to most
people in their eighties, but the problem with using specific categories such as third and fourth age is that the nature and rate of the
ageing process varies so much from person to person. The difference between the third and fourth age is far more a matter of health,
capacities and attitudes than of biological age as such. It is therefore impossible to link either category to a specific age-range, nor is
it easy to define exactly when the transition from third to fourth age

takes place. After all, for most people ageing involves a long and gradual transition, not a sudden step from one room to another.

While it remains unclear to what extent the phrases third and fourth age will ever come into general use, it is clear that a fundamental imbalance has emerged between the arduous middle years of life in which work and child-raising take place as opposed to the post-retirement years which are often filled with a surfeit of leisure. Young and middle-aged adults, women in particular, tend to have little free time because of the endless demands of work and child-raising. In contrast, many retirees suffer from having too much unstructured time on their hands. It is hardly surprising that among older people depression is so common that it has been described as 'the epidemic of old age'.[33] As the Carnegie Inquiry *Final Report* stated,

> being excluded from work and other purposeful activity can cause mental ill health ... We need to establish that the third age is not about retirement from activity into a long holiday, is not just about consumption, is not an apprenticeship for a fourth age of dependency ... Our society needs to develop a norm for continuing and changing activities, some paid and some not, for everyone for so long as health lasts.[34]

This problem has been described by Riley, Kahn and Foner as a structural lag which involves 'a mismatch between the strengths and potential capacities of the rising number of long-lived *people* and the lack of productive and meaningful *role opportunities*, or places in the social structure, that can foster, protect, and reward these strengths and capacities'.[35]

Various ways of dealing with the 'roleless role' of the later years have been proposed. Some writers have emphasised the value of education for older people; the late Peter Laslett even went so far as to claim that education in its widest connotation 'is the Third Age pursuit *par excellence*'.[36] Without doubt education can be deeply rewarding as well as providing valuable sociability; no one who has participated in continuing education courses in which most of the students were over sixty would deny how meaningful and liberating such courses can be. Yet as far as the elderly are concerned, continuing education is a minority pursuit and is likely to remain so. Retired people are only half as likely to participate in education as those who are employed or seeking work. In 1996 only 19 per cent of all 65 to 74 year olds were engaged in any form of education (formal or informal), a lower percentage than any younger cohort, and significant impediments to expansion of student numbers remain.[37] Continuing education lacks prestige and is seriously under-funded, part of the problem being the government's assumption that such education should lead to certificates or degrees and should therefore be funded on the basis of academic credit being granted to students who complete written assignments and examinations. Between 1990 and 1995 half of all local educational authorities actually cut their budgets for uncertificated adult education. Yet many older students enjoy class discussion as well as reading but are not particularly interested in undertaking lengthy written assignments in order to obtain formal academic credit. As Laslett quite rightly pointed out, 'highly disciplined inculcation, competitiveness, examinations, and so on' are, for the most part, out of place in the third age.[38]

While greater participation in continuing education would serve the needs of many older citizens, the possibility of continuing to work on a part-time basis probably has wider appeal. Retirement in its present incarnation is totally out of kilter with the nature of ageing. Retirement is a specific event which occurs on the day that employment ceases. In contrast, ageing is a very gradual process. It is unrealistic to conceive of most human beings as fit for full-time work one week but unfit for any further work immediately thereafter. Indeed, retirement can come as quite a shock, particularly for those without partners. Thus, a widowed nurse interviewed by researchers found retirement

> a traumatic experience. Well – suddenly – you have no company any more. At work you've got other people, lots of company, a lot of chat. And you miss that terribly ... You are alone and you just have to think of something to fill the day.[39]

Similarly, a factory supervisor who had been forced to retire at sixty-five commented that he had 'wanted to go on and on' but had no choice in the matter and afterwards felt 'very down ... I miss the complete involvement ... the responsibility, keeping your brain active. I miss the people I worked with.'[40]

One of the possible alternatives to total retirement is phased retirement, but this is not without difficulties of its own. Among the problems which older individuals may face in negotiating a transition from full to part-time work can be loss of power and responsibility, loss of status and markedly-reduced levels of compensation and benefits. Phased retirement has not become widely available, but employers have been taking a more flexible attitude towards the age at which retirement takes place. According to a 1996 Department for Education and Employment survey of 514 nationally representative employers in both the public and private sectors, 38 per cent of those employers had taken steps to make retirement provision more flexible and 13 per cent had actually raised the age of retirement.[41] Less than one-third of the employers retained a fixed age for retirement (see table 10.2).

Table 10.2 *Employers' retirement ages for men and women, 1996, Great Britain (%)*

	Men	Women
Fixed age	29	23
Flexible	42	48
No established age	22	22
Don't know	6	6

Sources: B. Hayward, S. Taylor, N. Smith and G. Davies, *Evaluation of the Campaign for Older Workers* (London: DEE, 1997), Chart 11. Based on a telephone survey of 514 organisations carried out by BMRB International in January and February 1996.

Despite apparent progress, it is not clear whether flexible retirement has been used by some employers to force (or encourage) employees to retire relatively early. What is clear is that in the face of ever-growing numbers of healthy retired people with not enough to do, there is much to be said for making both phased and flexible retirement readily-available options. Decades of aimless leisure do not, after all, provide a particularly satisfying conclusion to most lives.

Part IV

Redefining Britain

11

The new architecture

The fourth part of this book, Redefining Britain, will explore the impact of three developments which are not normally considered by social historians. Between 1950 and 2000 the character of life in Britain was profoundly affected by the international style of architecture, American culture and the growth of Britain's relationship with continental Europe. These three developments will be discussed in the next three chapters.

The international style

During the second half of the twentieth century, many of Britain's city centres were altered almost out of recognition. By the end of the century the city centres of Manchester and Birmingham bore little resemblance to their pre-war selves. This change was made possible by the post-war acceptance of a radical new architecture derived from foreign models.

Created on the continent during the 1920s and 1930s by Gropius, Le Corbusier and other architects of singular originality, what became known as the international style initially received a cautious if not positively chauvinistic reception in Britain. During the 1930s, European emigrés such as Mendelsohn, Chermayeff and Lubetkin attempted to import unalloyed continental modernism to Britain. They designed a number of imaginative and original structures such as Mendelsohn and Chermayeff's De La Warr Seaside Pavilion at Bexhill (1933–35), Lubetkin's graceful Penguin Pool at the London Zoo (1933–34) and his pioneering High Point Buildings in Highgate (1935 and 1938), but modernism was not embraced by most British-born architects until after the war. One of the reasons for this was the gentlemanly character of the higher reaches of the architectural profession in pre-war Britain. The Architectural Association, the preeminent source of training for the peaks of the profession, was located in suitably Georgian Bedford Square and drew almost all of its pupils from private schools, the purpose of the entrance interview being chiefly 'to determine whether your father's wallet was full enough'.[1] The Association's Director of Education until 1935, the influential Howard Robertson, was, it seems, 'a gentleman who expected to preside over "gentlemen"'.[2] Modernism, in contrast, was not class bound and had not grown out of the British past. In 1933 Sir Reginald Blomfield had said that modern architecture was 'essentially Continental in its origins and inspiration, and it claims as a merit that it is cosmopolitan. As an Englishman and proud of his country, I detest and despise cosmopolitanism'.[3]

The foreignness of the new architecture was not just a matter of its provenance but its fundamental character. Light was central. Large windows (and lots of them) were to admit as much light as possible and plain white interior surfaces were to reflect and reify that light. Brightness and whiteness were intimately associated with cleanliness, fresh starts and a rejection of history, the past being seen as tangled, dark, and dirty, much like the slums of the major European cities. Based on logical arguments and making full use of twentieth-century materials such as plate glass and reinforced concrete, the new architecture would, European architects claimed, help to bring about a new society. In philosophical terms modernism was rooted in continental idealism, and was thus at odds with Britain's far more empirical traditions. By deliberately stripping architecture of much of its language – adornment and colour in particular – and by rejecting historical references, the new style placed a premium on an architect's ability to handle form, volume and sequences of space. Much of the most original modern architecture could be viewed as sculpture, best displayed in a space large enough to isolate a building from its immediate surroundings. Indeed, following Le Corbusier some architects placed their buildings on stilts, thus creating an open space between building and site. Under such circumstances, choice of site and the nature of site development could markedly affect the appearance of a building.

Modernism remained very much a minority taste before the war, but radically-changed war-time conditions forced many British architects to work in new ways. During the war years, architects joined collaborative efforts to design and construct urgently-needed factories and hospitals and prefabrication came into vogue. Britain's need for massive rebuilding after the war also became a matter of great concern. As hostilities drew to a close, British architects and planners, buoyed by a desire to begin afresh and facing pressing social needs, finally began to espouse modernism. They did so partly because they believed that more efficient construction techniques would be made necessary by the sheer scale of post-war reconstruction. After all, Le Corbusier himself had espoused mass production.

During the years just after the war, many young architects with new ideas entered the profession and the balance of opinion began to shift rapidly. Seven of the ten architects elected to the Council of the Royal Institute of British Architects in 1950 were modernists.[4] By the end of the 1950s the international style had become the style of choice for most large new buildings in Britain. It would, however, be simplistic to portray those buildings as a single architectural entity. In considering post-war architecture there is much to be said for making clear distinctions between different types of building built in different surroundings to serve different purposes. Markedly dissimilar circumstances shaped the character of the relatively small number of buildings designed by architects of note for universities and other elite institutions as opposed to the far larger number of buildings designed to meet purely commercial specifications or provide public housing.

At the top of the architectural market, the planning of new universities in the 1960s presented a golden opportunity to a handful of highly-talented architects. Greenfield sites lacked historic context, so neither the juxtaposition of old and new architecture nor incompatibility of scale could become a problem. Moreover, on greenfield sites the hardness and anonymity of unadorned concrete and glass could be softened by surrounding expanses of landscape, either indigenous or newly-installed. Some of the most successful modern buildings of the 1960s were designed for new universities such as York and Sussex or for careful insertion within the ample grounds of the older universities. Probably the most conspicuously sculptural of these buildings were the curiously-shaped structures of Sir James Stirling, whose pioneering Engineering Building at Leicester (1963) was followed by his less successful Cambridge University History Faculty Building (1967), which has been difficult to heat and maintain. Stirling's remarkably idiosyncratic early buildings were designed to be seen in ample space, but other architects proved that it was possible to design highly original modern structures which complemented adjacent buildings of hallowed pedigree. Thus, Powell and Moya's student residence at Brasenose College (1961) and Picture Gallery at Christ Church (1968) were both beautifully-refined additions to highly confined sites.

In stark contrast, the cheek-by-jowl insertion of large modern commercial buildings in crowded city centres presented major problems of style, scale and land-use. Commercial considerations demanded the creation of maximum rentable floor space at minimum cost, and in most cases it was prohibitively expensive to acquire, develop and maintain more than negligible amounts of surrounding site. The result was a seemingly endless proliferation of anonymous office buildings which ignored life outside their well-guarded doors. Large office blocks with rows of identical rectangular windows looked much the same whether they happened to be in London, Manchester, Chicago or Sydney. Such buildings lacked the regional and historical associations of earlier buildings, yet failed to embody the deft and imaginative handling of form and volume so important to the most distinguished modern architecture. A few large office buildings had considerable architectural merit, such as the beautifully proportioned Economist Building in London (Alison and Peter Smithson, 1964), but for the most part architects had to build what commercial interests and local authorities wished to pay for.

Perhaps the most important problem posed by large commercial buildings involved scale. In order to maximise the amount of rentable space it was essential to design buildings which filled their sites and were relatively high. Constructing such buildings in Britain only became possible after restrictions on building licences were lifted. From 1945 until 1954 commercial building was largely limited to the repair and reconstruction of structures which had been damaged during the war. Moreover, Victorian legislation still limited the height of new buildings in London to eighty feet, thus preserving existing scale. After the war many cities developed plans which provided the basis for later construction, but only after the lifting of building restrictions did tall new buildings begin to alter the skylines of Britain's largest cities. The decade from 1954 to 1964 saw the construction in London of New Zealand House, the Shell Building, Millbank Tower and the Royal Garden Hotel, among others.[5] The problem of incompatible scale was not just a matter of high new buildings towering over low old buildings. During the working day large commercial buildings housed large numbers of employees, all of whom had to travel to and from work, so the city centre building boom went hand in hand with the construction of roads and multi-storey car parks. City centre after city centre was gutted to make way for commercial redevelopment schemes in which architectural quality was of little interest to those in control; any number of buildings replicated the more banal features of the international style (flat roofs, plain surfaces, no detail, and so on) while utterly failing to reproduce the austere elegance of the early modern masters.

The mania to build tall and large affected not only commercial construction but public housing, where the high rise was seen as a modern, cost-effective way to house millions of ordinary people. More than 200,000 homes had been destroyed during the war and another 250,000 had been made uninhabitable.[6] Moreover, millions of homes were in poor repair because little maintenance had been possible during the war years. To post-war architects, planners and local authorities, the best solution seemed to be to pull down damaged and decrepit houses and start afresh, a practice in keeping with the fundamental tenets of the modern movement. Given the political climate of the day and the poverty of many of those to be housed, the answer to Britain's pressing housing needs would be buildings built, owned and let by the state. A basic framework of law, money and advice would be provided by central government, but the actual planning and construction of public housing would be controlled by local authorities. Between 1945 and 1970 over four million public dwellings were completed, comprising 59 per cent of all housing construction in Britain.[7] It was a singular achievement, undertaken for the best of motives. Yet it produced mixed results. It would be inaccurate to suggest that during the 1950s and 1960s local authorities espoused the building of tower blocks at the expense of other forms of housing – far more low-rise buildings than tower blocks were built every year. The first public housing tower block was not completed until 1950 and between 1953 and 1959 high-rise flats represented only 9 per cent of building by local authorities. Only between 1963 and 1967 did approvals of tower blocks exceed 20 per cent of local authority construction, peaking at 26 per cent in 1966 before plummeting to 10 per cent by 1970, two years after the highly-publicised collapse of Ronan Point, a shoddily-built tower block in London's East End.[8]

Some of the reasons for building high-rise public housing were the same as the reasons for building high-rise commercial buildings. Tower blocks would make possible the most efficient use of expensive land and permit the concentration of services such as electricity and sewage on one site. Costs could also be contained by making use of system-building which facilitated rapid construction. Moreover, high buildings would be healthy to live in as their height and large windows would expose tenants to far more sunlight than flowed through the small windows of low-lying rows of grimy terrace houses. Light and cleanliness were, after all, central to the modern movement.

1 Ronan Point, Newham, London, after gas explosion in 1968

There were various arguments for high-rise construction, but it soon became clear that there were also major problems with public housing tower blocks and that those problems could not easily be solved. For one thing, to lift people high in the air was to uproot them. As Robert Hewison later wrote, 'the logic of the commercial skyscraper was applied to homes ... From the alienated heights of these structures people looked down on the empty wastes where their former homes had been, and turned back to watch *Coronation Street* on television'.[9] Other problems were less a matter of deficiencies in modernist architectural theory than of grossly inadequate public funding leading to shoddy construction, inadequate maintenance, and, in many cases, virtually non-existent development of surrounding sites. Poor materials and inexpensive methods of construction resulted in buildings which were noisy to live in and deteriorated rapidly. Deficient maintenance soon resulted in seedy hallways and inoperable elevators. Skimped site development meant that many buildings were surrounded not by well-kept greenery but by waste land. In addition, flawed social policy often resulted in failure to choose tenants with adequate care. Given the buildings' height and the lack of surrounding parkland, tower blocks were particularly ill-suited to families with young children; mothers could hardly supervise outdoor play from their windows and doorways high in the air. Crime and vandalism also became serious problems as lengthy unsupervised exterior walkways made burglary easy and long stretches of easily-accessible rendered wall invited graffiti. The problem was partly a matter of territory. Old terraced houses might be cramped and lack up-to-date kitchens and toilets but at least family domains were clear. In contrast, tower blocks contained long external walkways or internal corridors, elevators and surrounding

2 Tower blocks, Gorbals, Glasgow, surrounded by waste land

land which were neither under the protection of individual families nor adequately supervised by local authority employees.

The rejection of public housing tower blocks began in the late 1960s and increased rapidly thereafter. Few such buildings were designed after the 1960s, but by then about 1.5 million people were living in them. A study completed in 1985 showed that fully 45 per cent of Britain's 4,570 tower blocks belonged to the ten poorest local authorities, a situation which hardly contributed to standards of maintenance.[10] To ascribe the rejection of the public housing tower block solely to the problems already adumbrated would be to underestimate the extent to which the public imagination seized upon the tower block as a symbol of all it had come to dislike about modern architecture. Tower blocks were vilified not only because of what they were but because of what they were not. Monolithic and stark, they had little in common with more traditional forms of British housing. For one thing, it was impossible to live high above ground level and enjoy looking at or caring for an adjacent garden. Le Corbusier had envisioned the flat modern roof as a site for gardens and recreational facilities, and at his Unité d'Habitation in Marseilles such features became popular with the residents, but the raw British climate hardly made the windy roofs of tower blocks suitable venues for such use.

A significant part of the problem was not tower blocks as such but the character of the international style itself. Britons' highly-valued privacy was threatened by modernist design, with its emphasis on large windows and free-flow open-plan interiors. Neither privacy nor cosyness loomed large in the modernist vocabulary. Yet one of the central functions of most British houses was to protect and conceal domestic life from the world outside. The homes of the poor as well as the wealthy had long been essentially private domains, protected from intrusion not only by law and custom but by architectural plan. With boundaries to the side and rear carefully demarcated by hedges or walls, the classical town house was deliberately closed to the outside world, its front windows well above street level and its gardens invisible to passers-by. Privacy and cosiness were also provided by traditional cottage and pub interiors, with their small windows and open fireplaces. In contrast, large modern windows provided light and views but could also leave occupants feeling exposed and vulnerable. One could perhaps live in a glass-walled house with the curtains drawn, but why bother?

On the whole, Britons with the means to choose continued to prefer older houses or new houses built in traditional styles. From the start, the international style had faced a formidable barrier in Britain which it never managed to overcome as far as private housing was concerned. Given the immensely rich and varied architectural inheritance of private dwellings – from Georgian town houses to Victorian rectories to vernacular dwellings of all kinds – the very people who could have paid for houses in the modern style preferred to live in houses of historic provenance, preserving exteriors while gradually adapting interiors – kitchens and bathrooms in particular – to modern tastes and needs. For those with sufficient capital, lovely old houses and their gardens were widely available, and such houses had far more warmth and character than most newly-built structures. Most Britons wanted to feel that their houses had familiar qualities, so many of the new houses built by developers retained recognisably British styling cues such as neo-Victorian ornamental brick work or partially half-timbered facades superimposed on utterly conventional structures.

There were, of course, exceptions, but these remained the province of a tiny cognoscenti. As students of architecture in the late 1950s, Richard Rogers and Norman Foster met at Yale University where they both received graduate training. Shortly after returning to Britain they formed a partnership called Team Four, and one of their first projects was Creek Vean (1966), a house in Cornwall designed for Rogers' father-in-law. Over thirty years after its construction Creek Vean remains an unusual house. Set on a cliff-top overlooking the River Fal, the house rises out of the contours of its site like some of the buildings which Rogers had seen in California. Deyan Sudjic has commented that Creek Vean 'offers a spatial complexity and informality that seems closer to California than

Cornwall'.[11] Yet the architectural antecedents of Creek Vean were diverse, for while the house has open-plan rooms and a two-storey glass wall which offers spectacular views, it also has a turf roof, slate floors, and honey-coloured block walls, none of which are to be found in modern California houses.[12] Monumental in its exterior forms (despite the informality of its interior), Creek Vean is a house of considerable distinction. Yet it spawned few imitations. Rogers and Foster went on to design other houses, but their true vocations were to be fulfilled in far larger projects. Creek Vean is a minor masterpiece, an early work by two men who would go on to become world-renowned architects, but the house set no trends. Modernist houses can be found here and there in Britain, but there are not many of them because not many Britons wanted to live in them.

The international style drew considerable criticism during the 1970s, but the most damaging critique was not made until the following decade. In a speech celebrating the 150th anniversary of the Royal Institute of British Architects given in May 1984, Prince Charles profoundly unsettled leading architects by saying that 'it would be a tragedy if the character and skyline of our capital city were to be further ruined and St. Paul's dwarfed by yet another giant glass stump, better suited to downtown Chicago than the City of London' and, more pointedly, that the proposed new wing of the National Gallery looked like 'a monstrous carbuncle on the face of a much loved and elegant friend'.[13] In his subsequent film and book, *A Vision of Britain* (1989), Charles made it clear that he intensely disliked modernist architecture, writing,

> Above all, it seems to me that we have suffered too long from the imposition of a kind of nondescript, mediocre, synthetic, international style of architecture which is found everywhere – from Riyadh to Rangoon. Our own heritage of regional styles and individual characteristics has been eaten away by this creeping cancer, and I would suggest the time is ripe to rediscover the extraordinary richness of our architectural past.[14]

Charles did not merely dislike the international style; he demonised it. Le Corbusier was 'the notorious modernist architect and planner' and the fashionable architectural theories of the 1950s and 1960s had 'spawned deformed monsters which have come to haunt our towns and cities'.[15]

Behind Charles' hyperbole lurked a reasonable if not particularly original argument. He strongly objected to the size and impersonality of modernist city centre buildings with their disregard for historical context and their tendency to dwarf or obscure old buildings, including St Paul's. Charles passionately believed in limiting scale and creating community through a return to long-established principles and values which would be conveyed by traditional styles and materials.[16] But how was this to be achieved? Whether in Richmond or Dorchester, earnest fakes were not a particularly satisfactory response. Built adjacent to Dorchester on Duchy of Cornwall land under Charles' patronage, Poundbury conspicuously lacked the genuine eccentricities and irregularities (and, thus, the character) of a historic English town. Like Disneyland, Poundbury was much too clean. Surely there was much to be said for simply conserving historic buildings and districts rather than creating ersatz imitations. Conservation could not, however, provide more than a partial answer. In the final analysis neither the prince nor his country could evade the pressures of the late twentieth century. It was perhaps a sign of the times that *A Vision of Britain* had been published by the London subsidiary of an American firm and printed in Germany.

After modernism

One of the most consistent themes of this book has been the decline of orthodoxy and the rise of diversity, and those themes certainly characterise the history of British architecture after 1970. By the early 1970s the international style had begun to mutate and derivative styles had begun to appear. These styles all grew out of modernism and retained many of its features. Late twentieth-century materials, technologies and comforts were all here to stay, but the purity and simplicity of early modernism were increasingly sacrificed by hybrid styles which included historical references or else developed modernism into High-Tech forms. The phrase post-modern has been widely used to describe much of the new architecture, but remains problematic because it is so imprecise. The phrase is telling when used to describe the remarkably eclectic and deliberately ironic architecture which has been spawned by the ultimately rootless pan-historicism of the American Robert Venturi and his followers, who seem to regard the aesthetic past as a parts-bin, but the phrase is arguably less appropriate for other developments such as High Tech or neo-vernacular. Regardless of how the phrase post-modern is used, what is clear is that since about 1970 British architecture has become far more diverse.

The new diversity has not necessarily been radical in spirit, and neo-vernacular architecture has been a case in point. Modern architecture had been created by European architects of genius who wanted to plan how millions of people would live. It did not grow from popular demand. In contrast, by the 1970s the burgeoning urban conservation movement expressed widely-felt needs which increasingly received official support. The Town Planning Act of 1968 had provided for the designation of Conservation Areas and the Housing Act of 1969 provided increased funds for refurbishment. Urban conservation was not unrelated to what came to be known as gentrification – after all, no one sought to preserve slums as slums, no matter how antique they might be – and the desire to improve as well as protect historic town centres led not only to the rehabilitation of old buildings (often for new purposes), but to the designing of adjacent new buildings in what became known as the neo-vernacular style. The first involved modernising the old and the second involved designing the new to evoke the old, and the results were not totally dissimilar, at least as far as a pervasive brickyness was concerned. White surfaces and flat roofs had no nationality whereas brick and pitched roofs were seen as quintessentially English (brick could hardly be seen as quintessentially Scottish or Welsh). The fact that some of Alvar Aalto's finest buildings were in brick or that Bruges and Boston were no less bricky than Leeds or

London was somehow irrelevant. Brick was warm, familiar and reassuring, and unlike concrete it aged well. The late Raphael Samuel wrote of the numerous partisans of neo-vernacular that

> In recoil from the 'faceless' buildings of functionalist architecture, they invest brickwork with almost human qualities. It is tactile, textured and grainy where modernism's surfaces are flat. It is individual and quirky where modernism is uniform, 'warm' where glass and concrete are cold ... It grows old gracefully where curtain walling stains. Brick matures and improves with the passage of the years: modernism goes to seed.[17]

The apotheosis of brick was surely reached by the Hillingdon Civic Centre (Andrew Derbyshire, 1977), the most widely-praised neo-vernacular building of the 1970s. The Centre is a massive structure designed to house 1,300 local government staff and their clients. Nevertheless, Derbyshire deliberately designed it to be 'a building that spoke a language of form intelligible to its users (its occupants as well as the citizens of the borough) and used it to say something

3 Hillingdon Civic Centre, Hillingdon (Andrew Derbyshire of Matthew, Marshall, Johnson and Partners, 1977)

that they wanted to hear'.[18] To achieve this aim, he used soft red brick and tile on a grand scale, writing later that 'the use of cladding materials indigenous to the borough gives the building a familiar colour and texture and adds the infinitely variable surface which is characteristic of hand made things'.[19] Moreover, highly visible pitched roofs were intended to provide a 'protective, welcoming element'.[20] The building's fame resulted not from Derbyshire's use of traditional materials but from his using such materials in an extraordinary way, as pitched roofs of varying shapes, sizes and degrees of slant linked the numerous steps and bays which divided facades into patterns so complex that they only become legible when seen at a distance. The rough and highly variegated exterior of the Hillingdon Centre has nothing in common with the international style's flatness, smoothness and regularity.

The Hillingdon Centre was by no means the only truly original neo-vernacular building of the 1970s, but the style was to become popular in the considerably less complex forms favoured by

4 Hillingdon Civic Centre, Hillingdon (Andrew Derbyshire of Matthew, Marshall, Johnson and Partners, 1977)

developers of up-market homes, supermarkets and shopping malls, forms which tended to involve minor variations on a limited number of widely-accepted themes. One Sainsbury's resembles another just as one Tesco resembles another. Neo-vernacular offends no one, but reduced to its most common elements it has produced pleasant buildings which are anonymous simply because they look so much alike. Part of the problem may be that, as Raphael Samuel pointed out, neo-vernacular has been marketed as regional and local but much of it is actually international in character, neither brick nor pitched roofs being exactly unknown outside the United Kingdom.[21] Splendid as it is, the Hillingdon Centre could easily have been Flemish or Danish; it would be no less at home in, say, Copenhagen than it is in one of greater London's outlying boroughs.

Whereas neo-vernacular has become popular for homes and supermarkets, more eclectic styles have been widely-employed in the design of museums and commercial buildings. One of the best known examples of post-modern architecture in Britain is Robert Venturi's Sainsbury Wing of the National Gallery (1991). Venturi managed to solve the dilemma of how to build next to a very famous and very large building by combining Portland stone and classical columns with discontinuities and ambiguities which give the Sainsbury Wing an architectural identity of its own. The wing is quintessentially post-modern in its mixed signals: The classical columns of the facade abut a glass curtain wall; at the main entrance one encounters small fluted Egyptian columns which reappear in the foyer in floor-to-ceiling form; subsequently one ascends the stairs under large grey ornamental arches which appear to be Victorian in inspiration. These unexpected transitions are entertaining, but the interior is only partially satisfactory. The wide grand staircase with its fine views of Trafalgar Square sweeps upwards to culminate in the entry to an elevator. The rooms themselves are considerably smaller than the major rooms of the National Gallery, and their relative smallness reminds one that the wing is ultimately an adjunct to a much larger building on a much larger site. Fewer but larger rooms might have been less claustrophobic.

Charles Jencks has written that 'the content of so much Post-Modernism is the past seen with irony or displacement'.[22] This is certainly true of the Sainsbury Wing and hundreds of other post-modern buildings, but it is not *necessarily* true of the style. It is not obligatory to take history with a grain of salt, and the profoundly original buildings of Richard MacCormac provide a case in point. MacCormac's buildings pay homage to some of the great masters of English architecture. The prospect towers of his Bowra Building at Wadham College (1992) deliberately echo the bold, confident towers of Robert Smythson's Hardwick Hall, as do the towers which MacCormac subsequently designed for his Garden Quadrangle at St John's (1993). One of the most important buildings of the 1990s, the complex and highly-sophisticated Garden Quadrangle also pays tribute to Soane's Bank of England in the elliptical curves of its saucer-domed semi-subterranean and deliberately grotto-like public rooms. MacCormac's singular achievement has been to create

5 The Sainsbury Wing of the National Gallery, London (Robert Venturi, 1991). Classical columns abut a glass curtain wall

6 The Sainsbury Wing
of the National Gallery,
London (Robert
Venturi, 1991). Entry
staircase beneath non-
structural decorative
arches

elegant modern buildings which summon with reverence the spirits
of their architectural ancestors, yet manage to do so without pastiche.
He has said that he believes it is possible to 'engage with architectural
memories in a way that is not superficial' and that 'one can penetrate
history without being a slave to a stylistic trap'.[23] In this he succeeds;
MacCormac's buildings are ultimately mysterious, and deliberately
so, partly because his enthusiasm for contrasting bold towers with
concealed lower regions helps to make it impossible to view most of
his buildings as a whole. Inside or outside, high or low, what one sees
depends on one's vantage point. MacCormac's buildings are certainly post-modern in their sense of the fluidity of possibility, yet the

central role played by English references grounds them in a way which is rare among post-modern buildings.

On first consideration, neither Derbyshire's Hillingdon Centre nor Venturi's Sainsbury Wing nor MacCormac's Garden Quadrangle would seem to have much in common with each other, let alone with the most famous British building of the last fifteen years of the twentieth century, Sir Richard Rogers' Lloyd's Building in London (1986). Like Rogers' earlier Pompidou Centre, the Lloyd's Building involves an extravagant display of what has come to be known as High Tech. High Tech has involved the mutation of modernism into an extreme (and highly expensive) form.

7 Hardwick Hall, Derbyshire (Robert Smythson, 1590–96)

8 Garden Quadrangle,
St John's College,
Oxford (MacCormac,
Jamieson and
Pritchard, 1993)

9 Bowra Building, Wadham College, Oxford (MacComac, Jamieson and Pritchard, 1992)

10 The Lloyd's
Building, London
(Richard Rogers and
Partners, 1986).
Exterior view of the
atrium and towers

Lacking the international style's simplicity and cleanness of line, High Tech celebrates technology by turning buildings inside out, exposing both structure and services (elevators, escalators, pipes, and much else) to public view. High Tech's emphasis on transparency helps to transform elevators and escalators from necessary but mundane features into highly visible moving parts of the architecture itself. Who would not stop to gaze with awe and a bit of trepidation at the external elevators which endlessly slide up and down the soaring outer walls of Lloyd's?

Yet the Lloyd's Building celebrates more than technology and process alone. The building's skyline, replete with cranes which

11 The Lloyd's
Building, London
(Richard Rogers and
Partners, 1986).
Façade detail

become bird-like in silhouette, can be seen as monumental sculpture and Lloyd's central atrium is a cross between a cathedral transept and the Crystal Palace. Moreover, the highly irregular ground-floor exterior of the building, with its outdoor terrace and open stairs, engages passers-by and provides a lively interface between Lloyd's and nearby buildings. Like I. M. Pei's East Building of the National Gallery of Art in Washington (1978) and Louvre Pyramids in Paris (1983–88), the Lloyd's Building explodes the myth that a building must resemble its neighbours if it is not to clash with them.

In many respects, the Hillingdon Centre, Sainsbury Wing, Garden Quadrangle and Lloyd's Building have little in common;

they are very different buildings built on very different sites to serve the needs of very different clients. Yet for all their dissimilarities, the buildings do share certain virtues. The international style stood accused of rejecting the past, ignoring context, and being insensitive to users' needs. In contrast, the Hillingdon Centre, Sainsbury Wing, Garden Quadrangle and Lloyd's Building ignore neither client nor setting. Each building was designed with enormous care to serve specific needs, and each holds a dialogue with its surroundings and with the architectural past. None of these four buildings could be justly accused of ignoring its context.

On the other hand, the obvious differences between these four buildings provide a fine example of the most important facet of British architecture during the last twenty-five years of the twentieth century, namely the absence of orthodoxy. The lack of a dominant theme opened up marvellous opportunities for architects to develop their own visions, and it is important that the use of stylistic name-tags not be allowed to obscure the individuality and originality of the results. If architecture reflects the values of a society (or, at least, the tastes of those who pay for buildings), late twentieth-century architecture certainly reflected the diversity of late twentieth-century Britain. Diversity is not conducive to consistent standards, but it is surely inimical to dullness of soul.

12

Living in the American age

It would be hard to over-estimate the diversity of American influences on British life during the second half of the twentieth century. From words and phrases to films to music to business to education to computers to scientific research, American models became so omni-present and so influential that it would take a substantial monograph indeed to investigate the scope of their impact. The difficulty in assessing the effects of American culture stems not only from the sheer diversity of what has been involved but from there being so many instances in which it is not possible to make a clear distinction between American culture *per se* as opposed to trends which have come to pervade the modern world. For example, from Apple to IBM to Hewlett Packard to almighty Microsoft, American companies have flooded the world with computer design and technology. There is no British Bill Gates. Yet computer components are manufactured in any number of countries and the use of PCs has become so universal that it would be simplistic to portray the newly-important role of the computer in British life as simply an example of American influence.

Another problem in writing a relatively brief analysis of the impact of American culture on life in post-war Britain is that the advent of American influence was hardly a post-war development – after all, Britons were hoovering their carpets, eating Kellogg's Corn Flakes and driving Fords long before the war. By 1920 fully two-thirds of all cars sold in Britain were Model-T Fords, and after sales fell sharply due to a 33⅓ per cent duty Ford purchased land at Dagenham on which it built the largest car factory outside the United States. Similarly, General Motors purchased Vauxhall in 1927 and American tyre manufacturers such as Firestone and Goodyear also built factories in Britain.[1]

By 1934, in *English Journey,* J. B. Priestley could write of what he had seen between Southampton and Romsey that

> this road, with its new lock-up shops, its picture theatres, it red-brick little villas, might have been anywhere: it is the standard new suburban road of our time, and there are hundreds of them everywhere, all alike. Moreover, they only differ in a few minor details from a few thousand such roads in the United States, where the same tooth-pastes and soaps and gramophone records are being sold, the very same films are being shown.[2]

By the mid-1950s life had moved on, so much so that Priestley and Jacquetta Hawkes could write in *Journey Down a Rainbow* (1957) that

> We are already in another age, when America mostly pays the piper and calls for most of the tunes. There is no longer any point in leaving Leicester Square and Coventry Street in order to describe Broadway, which merely has more electric light, newer Hollywood films, larger cafeterias. English readers have not to be conducted across the Atlantic now to observe the American style of urban life: it can be discovered in the nearest town. It is now the great invader.[3]

Priestley and Hawkes exaggerated, but they were hardly alone in fearing the homogenising potential of American influence. In *The Uses of Literacy,* also published in 1957, Richard Hoggart turned the newly-popular milk-bar into a symbol of cultural decay, writing,

> milk-bars indicate at once, in the nastiness of their modernistic knick-knacks, their glaring showiness, an aesthetic breakdown ... most of the customers are boys aged between fifteen and twenty, with drape-suits, picture ties and an American slouch. Most of them cannot afford a succession of milk-shakes, and make cups of tea serve for an hour or two whilst – and this is their main reason for coming – they put copper after copper into the mechanical record player. About a dozen records are available ... almost all are American ... The young men waggle one shoulder or stare, as desperately as Humphrey Bogart, across the tubular chairs.
>
> Compared even with the pub around the corner, this is all a peculiarly thin and pallid form of dissipation, a sort of spiritual dry-rot amid the odour of boiled milk. Many of the customers – their

clothes, their hair-styles, their facial expressions all indicate – are living to a large extent in a myth-world compounded of a few simple elements which they take to be those of American life.[4]

Hoggart was right about inauthenticity. Real Americans rarely boil milk, nor do they down a succession of milk-shakes as if they were quaffing pints of beer – in this respect Hoggart may have confused the milk-bar with a pub. Details aside, Hoggart's portrait of wistful 1950s working-class youths was uncharitable, to say the least. They were, after all, only waiting for the 1960s to arrive.

The central concern of Priestley, Hoggart, and others was that imported American culture would foster a soul-deadening uniformity. The proliferation of mass-produced goods and pseudo-American habits would be antithetical to the individuality and idiosyncrasy of national, regional and local life, and Britain might well be swamped by the far larger and wealthier society which had come to see itself as a model for the western world. In John Osborne's *Look Back in Anger* (1957), Jimmy Porter says 'I must say it's pretty dreary living in the American Age – unless you're an American of course. Perhaps all our children will be Americans. That's a thought isn't it?'[5]

Jimmy Porter was not alone. In *The American Invasion* (1962), Francis Williams warned that

> The impact of American ideas, and still more of American ways of life, is now so large, the drive of America to Americanise so great, that to ask how much of what is specifically English in our civilisation will remain in a decade or two if the trend continues is by no means absurd.[6]

Williams knew the United States well and believed that

> the best of American life, like the best of English or French life, is not for export. What too often moves across the world in the wake of American money and American know-how is what is most brash and superficial; a surface way of life which although truly and overpoweringly American derives not from the deeper virtues of American character but from those influences which have most markedly shaped it in the public domain.[7]

Concern about the impact of American culture on British life was not limited to intellectuals such as Osborne and Williams. Part of the concern stemmed from ordinary Britons' conceptions of what Americans were like. In April 1947, Mass Observation claimed with regard to Britons' views of Americans that

> There arise two sharply contrasting and yet fundamentally similar groups of opinion. In the one the American is immature emotionally and intellectually; he is boastful and flamboyant, bad mannered and full of intolerance to any minority group. But in the other he is simple and ingenuous, impulsive and uninhibited, friendly, kind-hearted and generous. In either case his likeness to a child is stressed with notable frequency.[8]

Such stereotypes reflected considerable ambivalence not only about American traits but about Britons' view of themselves. As Harry Hopkins wrote in 1964,

> Might it not, after all, merely be that we were old and weary and they were young and vital and full of the joy of living! That their society was adapted to the times it had played so large a part in forming, while ours was obsolescent, fatally weighed down under the burden of its glorious past? That this, in short, was more than ever the American Century?[9]

Whether or not the oft-used phrase American century is appropriate – and the case can be argued either way – the United States certainly was remarkably successful in many ways and American cultural influence was not about to disappear. Indeed, it was to grow stronger with the passing decades. Yet in some respects the nature of that influence was to change.

During the 1950s and 1960s, American cultural influence on British life was primarily felt in terms of films, pop music and conventional consumer goods. What was not apparent at the time was the extent to which the United States, a restless nation with a profound belief in education and progress, would grow more sophisticated and would export the results. By the 1980s and 1990s, Coca

Cola, Big Macs and sweat shirts with slogans had become artefacts of a cultural stratum over which a new layer of less down-market goods and tastes was being superimposed. From blueberry muffins to jambalaya, American food became increasingly popular; by the late 1990s Sainsbury's was practically awash with cranberry juice. The pseudo-American milk-bar dwindled into distant memory as Haagen-Dazs cafes and Seattle-style coffee-houses proliferated in British city centres. As to clothing, ever-more leisure wear of the kind sold by up-market American firms such as L. L. Bean, Eddie Bauer and Lands' End was now sold by a rapidly-multiplying cohort of British imitators such as Boden's, Racing Green and Hawkshead. Such clothing did not long remain the preserve of mail order firms alone; in 1996 Debenham's began to devote an entire subsection of each of its eighty-eight stores to a new line of clothing which involved a well-calculated take on the L. L. Bean look. The logo 'Maine New England' was sewn onto a wide range of specially-designed weatherproof shells, woolly jumpers and polo shirts which had actually been manufactured in Hong Kong, Macau and China. Debenham's highly visible display of its Maine New England brand was based on the correct assumption that its customers not only wished to dress like Americans but would be pleased to advertise the fact.

Another factor which changed with the passing of time was that from Avis to Visa, American brands and styles of shopping became so well-established that they came to seem a normal part of British life. The first supermarket had opened in the United States in 1923 whereas the first British supermarkets did not open until the early 1950s, but by 1958 there were 175 supermarkets in Britain and by 1967 there were 2,803.[10] By the 1980s and 1990s not just super-markets as such but the entire relocation of shopping to edge-of-town superstores reflected American trends and brought with it the very real danger of replicating the shabby, impoverished city centres so common in the United States.

Just as American-style consumer goods sold in Britain became more diverse, so a similar broadening of British taste took place in the arts. For example, an increasingly wide range of American music became familiar to British ears. By the late 1990s the works of Bernstein, Copland and Samuel Barber had become almost as familiar as those of Elgar to the five million Britons who listened to Classic FM.[11] Moreover, British performers of American music no longer restricted themselves to main-stream jazz, rock and popular classics; performances of American music now ranged from the works of Charles Ives and John Cage to formerly-obscure regional folk songs. During the mid-1990s, Radio 2 broadcast a weekly half hour of Cajun music largely sung by Britons who managed to reproduce Cajun French with apparent accuracy. There tended, however, to be a lack of reciprocity in such matters; it seemed unlikely that deep in the bayous Cajuns were practising morris dancing or that middle-brow Americans had taken to humming Elgar.

The growing variety of American-influenced tastes and styles was matched by Britons' increasingly accurate understanding of the sheer diversity of the United States itself. In the 1950s and 1960s very few Britons had ever crossed the Atlantic, an expensive journey largely available only to diplomats and the seriously rich. At the time, most Britons' image of the United States involved simplistic impressions gained from American television programs and films, which by the 1950s took up fully 70 per cent of British cinema projection time.[12] In contrast, by the 1980s and 1990s the combination of greater British prosperity and a temporarily advantageous exchange rate led to transatlantic forays becoming a common occurrence, as middle-class Britons began to view the United States as a possible holiday destination. The fact that hotel rooms, meals and consumer goods were all much less expensive on the other side of the Atlantic was part of the attraction. As recently as 1971 Britons took only 42,010 holidays in the United States, but by 2000 they took 2,569,000, an enormous increase.[13]

However it was acquired, more ample knowledge of American life did not necessarily result in unadulterated approbation. Indeed, such knowledge was apt to give Britons the pleasure of feeling some degree of moral superiority. The United States' lack of effective gun control and appallingly high homicide rate, the chasm between its haves and have-nots and its inordinate consumption of energy could all be unfavourably contrasted with Britain's somewhat more enlightened record in such matters. On the other hand, a wide variety of American practices such as management by objectives, self-assessed tax returns and city mayors with real power were deemed worthy of emulation. Many other instances could be cited. For example, as a result of the policies of the Higher Education Funding Council, Oxford University began to produce an annual Mission Statement and Strategic Plan, just like any American state university. In other instances, however, it was not easy to know whether American models were being consciously copied or not. For example, the end of the binary divide between British universities and polytechnics in 1991 made British higher education much more like American higher education in that the word university was applied to a far wider variety of institutions, but it is not obvious whether deliberate emulation of American higher education was involved.

In some instances attempts to import American ways of doing things initially aroused considerable misgivings. This was particularly true of the British response to American business methods. As Nick Tiratsoo has pointed out, during the 1950s American business methods were still viewed by British businessmen with scepticism and distaste. At the time there was still a gulf between American and British styles of management. American businesses valued consultation and teamwork and expected senior managers to have academic and technical qualifications. In contrast, large British firms were often led by charismatic but autocratic chief executives who had no formal business training and who dominated rigid hierarchies which were symbolised by as many as six or seven levels of restaurant and canteen.[14] As Tiratsoo has written of the British response to American business techniques during the 1950s, British employers

> resented being told to treat workers more seriously and worried about the American emphasis on management. Their fear here was that those who were really just servants of the firm might get ideas

above their station. Few had much sympathy for the American emphasis on discussion and the exchange of information. British firms had traditionally been secretive and it was still generally believed that all commercially sensitive data should remain closely guarded.[15]

This emphasis on secrecy, hierarchy and separate cultures within the workplace did much to foster the antipathies which fed the trade union militancy of the 1970s and eventually led to the backlash of the Thatcher era. It would be naive to suggest that British business practices changed utterly thereafter, but it is clear that American and Japanese methods – both of which emphasise the importance of consultation – gained acceptance as management training finally became more widely available in Britain. Some of the most influential business schools in the United States had been founded in the late nineteenth and early twentieth centuries: the Wharton School of Finance was founded in 1881, the University of Chicago Business School in 1898 and the Harvard Business School in 1908. In contrast, MBA programmes were not offered in the UK until the mid-1960s, but by the 1990s there were about 100 of them.

It would be wrong to suggest that by the end of the century large British businesses had all been transformed by eager MBAs. After all, British businesses continued to vary greatly and firms such as Rolls-Royce and Morgan continued to offer labour-intensive handcrafted products to niche markets. On the other hand, from the erosion of once-rigid union demarcations to the delayering of management hierarchies to ever-more use of the computer to a new-found dedication to pleasing customers, many British businesses had changed enormously. How much of this had to do with American influence as opposed to the iron hand of economic necessity and the increasingly global nature of the economic context is impossible to say.

All in all, by the late 1990s Britain's cultural and commercial relationship with the United States had become a relatively settled affair. Britons were no longer particularly worried about being overwhelmed by the new Rome, such fears having been replaced by concerns about the possible effects of ever-wider involvement in the European Union. Anglo-American cultural relations were not a major political issue whereas the question of whether to join the European Monetary Union had deeply divided the Conservative Party and had been one of the most important factors behind that party's resounding defeat in 1997. Not all Britons felt comfortable with American influence, but it had come to be accepted as a fact of life in a way that full participation in the European Union had not.

13

The ambivalent Europeans

Historians often portray the past in terms of progress or decline – the rise or fall (or rise and fall) of individuals, movements and nations are all classic historical themes. A conventional model of this ilk would not do justice to the halting evolution of Britain's relationship with continental Europe during the second half of the twentieth century. Britain's relationship with what was established in 1952 as the European Coal and Steel Community and eventually became the European Union was characterised by deep reservations which accurately reflected Britons' ambivalence as to whether they wished to see themselves as Europeans or as islanders whose closest affinities were with the Commonwealth and the United States. The titles of some of the histories of Britain's role in the European Community such as Roger Jowell and James Spence's *The Grudging Europeans* (1975), Stephen George's *An Awkward Partner* (1990) and David Gowland and Arthur Turner's *Reluctant Europeans* (2000) accurately reflected Britain's half-hearted embrace of its European neighbours; no one could have written a history of this topic and called it *Enthusiastic Europeans*.[1]

It would not be appropriate for this chapter to provide more than a fairly brief account of Britain's political and economic relationship with continental Europe between 1950 and 2000. What will be explored in some detail is how that relationship affected and reflected Britons' evolving sense of their place in the world. Given the remarkably unstable character of British public opinion with regard to membership of the European Community, it is important to make a clear distinction between what economists call secular trends as opposed to sharp but short-term swings in public mood and perception.

During the early 1950s few Britons had any reason to be particularly interested in the newly-formed European Coal and Steel Community, which had been founded primarily to serve French and German interests. On 9 May 1950, the French Foreign Minister Robert Schuman had announced that the French government proposed to 'place all French and German production of coal and steel under a common High Authority in an organisation open to the participation of other European countries'. The establishment of common bases of production would make 'all war between France and Germany not only unthinkable but physically impossible' and would lay 'the first concrete foundations for a European federation indispensable for preserving the peace'.[2] Jean Monnet, who drafted the Schuman Plan, had selected coal and steel as a basis for Franco-German cooperation because they had so recently been the basis of war production and were therefore of enormous psychological as well as practical significance. Having been occupied by German military forces for five traumatic years, the French deeply needed to develop a means of ensuring against any future German attempt at European hegemony. The Germans, on the other hand, were hardly Europe's most popular nation and desperately needed acceptance and respectability.[3] The founding of the European Coal and Steel Community in 1952 led directly to the Treaties of Rome of 1957 which established the European Economic Community.

Britain had been invited to join the ECSC but chose not to do so. There were a number of reasons for this. At the beginning of the 1950s Britain still saw itself as a global power for whom a strongly European identity would be too parochial. After all, Britain's industrial output and foreign trade were as large as those of France and Germany combined. Moreover, neither France nor Germany was regarded as a particularly desirable partner. Germany had recently been the national enemy whose Nazi government had been responsible for the deliberate murder of millions of innocent civilians. France, on the other hand, had long suffered from chronic political instability not to mention a striking inability to defend itself against German aggression. In March 1948, Ernest Bevin and Sir Stafford

Cripps had warned their Cabinet colleagues against 'associating ourselves with partners in Western Europe whose political condition is unstable and whose actions may be embarrassing to us'.[4]

In contrast, the United States and the Commonwealth had been indispensable war-time allies. At the beginning of the 1950s Britain still saw its primary international role as leader of the Commonwealth and partner of the United States. Leadership of the Commonwealth was seen as providing Britain with a world role of far greater significance than participation on an equal basis with economically inferior and potentially unreliable European partners. Moreover, in the early 1950s only 13 per cent of British exports went to the countries which were to form the European Economic Community whereas 47 per cent of British exports went to Commonwealth countries.[5] Trade aside, most Australians and New Zealanders, the majority of Canadians, and English-speaking South Africans were regarded by Britons as kith and kin. As a Labour Party pamphlet put it in 1950, 'In every respect except distance we in Britain are closer to our kinsmen in Australia and New Zealand on the far side of the world than we are to Europe. We are closer in language and in origins, in social habits and institutions, in political outlook and in economic interest.'[6]

During the 1950s most Britons had remarkably little knowledge of European affairs. A September 1957 Gallup Poll reported that 39 per cent of respondents had neither read nor heard about the European Common Market and that of those who had only 35 per cent knew that France was a member, 27 per cent knew that Germany was a member, and 20 per cent were under the impression that Britain was also a member. Three years later, only 49 per cent of Gallup Poll respondents had 'read or heard anything about the European Common Market'.[7] In contrast, there was strong public attachment to the Commonwealth. In September 1961 a Gallup Poll asked whether Europe, the Commonwealth or America was the most important to Britain, and 48 per cent of respondents chose the Commonwealth, 19 per cent chose America and only 18 per cent chose Europe, with 15 per cent undecided.[8] It is hardly surprising that at the end of July 1961, when Harold MacMillan announced that his government intended to negotiate for membership of the EEC, only 40 per cent of respondents to a Gallup Poll favoured joining.[9]

MacMillan's decision to seek EEC membership resulted from a growing realisation that European economic growth was outpacing that of Britain and that the Commonwealth was providing a declining proportion of the market for British exports. This decline had been so rapid that by 1961 Britain was already exporting more to Europe than to the Commonwealth. Moreover, membership of the European Free Trade Association of non-EEC countries had not proved to be a viable alternative to full membership of the EEC. President de Gaulle realised that Britain's change of policy was rooted in economic calculations and did not represent a fundamental change of self-definition. A fervent nationalist himself, de Gaulle understood full well Britain's pride in its global role. He was particularly unhappy with Britain's continuing to demand special treatment for most of the Commonwealth, primarily because unlike the UK France was a major agricultural producer and did not want to face competition from less expensive Commonwealth exports. On 14 January 1963, de Gaulle announced his veto of Britain's application, saying,

> England in effect is insular, she is maritime, she is linked through her exchanges, her markets, her supply lines to the most diverse and often the most distant countries ... What is to be done in order that England, as she lives, produces and trades, can be incorporated into the Common Market, as it has been conceived and as it functions? For example, the means by which the people of Great Britain are fed and which are in fact the importation of foodstuffs bought cheaply in the two Americas and in the former dominions, at the same time giving, granting [*sic*] considerable subsidies to English farmers? These means are obviously incompatible with the system which the Six have established quite naturally for themselves.[10]

Above all, de Gaulle feared that Britain's close links with the United States would lead to Britain becoming America's Trojan horse within the EEC. After the existing Common Market was enlarged to include EFTA members 'ultimately it would appear as a colossal Atlantic community under American dependence and direction, and which would quickly have absorbed the community of Europe'.[11]

As far as the British public was concerned, it was one thing to be disinclined to join but quite another to be snubbed, and de Gaulle's veto reinforced the very attitudes to which he objected. A 1965 Gallup Poll elicited a striking response to the question asked in table 13.1.

Table 13.1 *'Which other countries do you regard as Britain's friends?'*, *January 1965 (%)*

USA	73
Australia	57
Canada	48
Scandinavia	22
Holland	17
France	14
India	13
Switzerland	10
Belgium	9
West Germany	9
Italy	4
USSR	4
Austria	3
Others	22

Source: *Gallup Political Index*, nos 60 and 93 as cited in R. J. Shepherd, *Public Opinion and European Integration* (Farnborough: Lexington, 1975), Table 4.12, p. 89.

In November 1967, President de Gaulle vetoed a new application for membership by the Wilson government and during the next three years British public support for EEC membership collapsed. Between 1960 and 1971, successive Gallup Polls asked two slightly different questions: 'If the British government were to decide that Britain's interest would best be served by joining the European Common Market, would you approve or disapprove?' (1960–67) and 'Do you approve or disapprove of the Government applying for membership of the European Common Market?' (1967–71). The proportion of respondents who approved of joining sank from 49 per cent in July 1960 to only 16 per cent in November 1970, whereas the proportion who disapproved rose from a mere 13 per cent in July 1960 to 66 per cent in November 1970.[12] By 1970 Britons were strongly against joining the Common Market. Their chief concern was not so much potential loss of sovereignty as the threat of higher food prices. In October 1970 fully 73 per cent of Gallup Poll respondents believed that joining the Common Market would result in food prices rising 'a lot', whereas only 9 per cent had thought so in September 1961. This fear was by no means unreasonable, for according to government estimates made in 1970 the subsidies paid to European food producers would raise British food prices by 18 to 26 per cent.[13]

On the other hand, the politics of the situation were changing rapidly. After President de Gaulle resigned in 1969, Britain's diplomatic relationship with Europe had entered a completely new phase. In June 1970 Edward Heath, a fervent pro-European with little affection for the Commonwealth, reopened negotiations for British entry to the EEC. After almost three years of very hard work Britain became a member on 1 January 1973. There was, however, no popular mandate for joining. Not until 1975 was public approval finally obtained, a curious sequence of events. In the early 1970s public opinion was still thoroughly divided with regard to the wisdom of joining the EEC, yet in the June 1975 referendum in which about twenty-six million votes were cast, 67 per cent voted in favour of remaining in the EEC whereas only 33 per cent favoured leaving.[14] At first glance it would appear that a seismic shift in public opinion suddenly took place, but this was not the case. What occurred was a striking but short-lived shift in voters' calculations. Starting in 1973, British attitudes towards membership of the Common Market were measured by *Eurobarometer* surveys which asked the question in table 13.2.

Viewed in this context, the dramatic results of the 1975 referendum reflected a temporary surge of support, not a secular trend;

Table 13.2 *'Generally speaking, do you think that the UK's membership of the Common Market is a good thing, a bad thing, or neither good nor bad?'* *1973–91 (%)*

	1973	1975	1977	1979	1981	1983	1985	1987	1989	1991
Good thing	31	47	35	33	24	28	37	43	48	57
Bad thing	34	21	40	34	48	36	30	26	21	15
Neither good nor bad	22	19	22	26	24	29	28	25	26	–
No opinion	13	13	13	7	4	7	5	6	5	–

Sources: *Eurobarometer* surveys as cited in N. Nugent, 'British Public Opinion and the European Community' in S. George (ed.), *Britain and the European Community* (Oxford: Clarendon Press, 1992), Table 8.4, p.181 and *Eurobarometer*, no. 36 (Luxembourg: Office for Official Publications of the European Communities, December 1991), Figure 1.6, p. 14.

in 1975 twice as many survey respondents felt that membership was a good thing as a bad thing, but by 1981 twice as many respondents had come to feel that membership was a bad thing, although by 1991 57 per cent had decided that membership was a good thing after all and only 15 per cent continued to believe that it was a bad thing!

As far as membership of the EEC was concerned, British public opinion was remarkably volatile and apparently significant trends were reversed with almost predictable regularity. The fact that such a large proportion of Britons expressed different views at different times suggested that those views were not deeply held. For one thing, Britons did not necessarily attach great importance to EEC membership; in 1974 only 33 per cent believed that whether Britain remained in the EEC was very important and the majority of Britons continued to prefer Commonwealth ties.[15] Fully 67 per cent believed that 'Britain should have developed links with the Commonwealth rather than joined the Common Market' and 64 per cent agreed that 'the Commonwealth nations are better friends to Britain than the French, Germans or anybody in Western Europe will ever be'.[16] Given such opinions, the results of the 1975

Referendum were not so much a ringing endorsement of membership as a resigned acceptance of the new *status quo* made possible by three developments. First, in the previous two years world commodity prices had soared, reaching and in some cases exceeding European levels, so dear food could no longer be blamed on the Common Market. Second, after the Wilson government announced in March 1975 that it recommended Britain's staying in the EEC, many Labour supporters changed their minds and decided to support membership even though their party remained split on the issue. Wilson and Callaghan were far more popular than leading Labour anti-Europeans such as Benn, Foot and Shore, and many of the government's supporters did not wish to undermine its policies, particularly as the government had a majority of only three seats.[17] Third, the pro-Europeans had far more money to spend than the antis. This was hardly an accident, for according to a poll organised by *The Times* 415 of 419 company chairmen believed that Britain should remain in the EEC.[18] Britain in Europe, the umbrella group which ran the Yes campaign, was supported by the Confederation of British Industries as well as some important trade unions, and was far more successful at fund-raising than the poorly-organised No campaign. Finally, most newspapers supported the Yes campaign.

One of the most fundamental problems with joining and, later, supporting membership of the EEC was that the central argument for doing so was based on economic self-interest. That argument was technical in nature and had little to do with Britons' sense of themselves. It was not easy for white Britons to identify with continental Europeans in the way that they could identify with Australians, New Zealanders, Canadians or Americans. For one thing, continental Europeans spoke their own languages. Not many Britons were sufficiently fluent in French, German or Italian to conduct business or professional affairs in those languages, and language was the most important factor which made continental Europeans 'them' rather than 'us.' In contrast, members of the Commonwealth often had a British-style education and Americans regarded Shakespeare and Dickens not as foreign authors but as contributors to their own cultural heritage. At a more mundane level, ordinary Britons could easily identify with the characters in American films and Australian soaps. In contrast, there were many superb French films but these appealed to an educated minority; films with subtitles lacked mass market appeal and did not make for popular television viewing. Francois Truffaut, Louis Malle, Jean-Luc Goddard and Bertrand Tavernier all made wonderful films, but how many Britons actually saw them? For that matter, *Heimat* aside, German television simply did not exist as far as British viewers were concerned.

Under these circumstances there remained a wide gap between economic self-interest and national and personal identity. Most Britons did not, after all, think of themselves as Europeans. A 1990 *Eurobarometer* poll asked the question in table 13.3. The fact that most Britons did not see themselves as Europeans made it easy for them to regard the EEC as an association of foreigners.

Table 13.3 '*Do you ever think of yourself as not only [nationality] but also European?*', 1990 (%)

	Italy	France	Germany	UK
Often	20	19	12	12
Sometimes	37	38	27	16
Never	43	41	53	71
No reply	1	2	7	1

Source: *Eurobarometer*, no. 33, June 1990, p. 2.

Despite such problems, at least four long-term trends worked in favour of pro-EEC sentiment. To begin with, during the 1970s and 1980s the relative importance of the Commonwealth continued to decline. In the face of adamant French–Canadian nationalism, Canada was in no position to emphasise its British heritage, and stressed its multi-cultural character instead. Australians too were acquiring a much stronger sense of their own inimitable identity.

Moreover, the character of the entire Commonwealth was altered considerably by the admission of far more African and Asian nations. Of the 54 countries which belonged to the Commonwealth at the end of 1998, 33 were republics and only 15 recognised the Queen as their head of state. Such developments affected Britons' attitudes. In response to a June 1989 Gallup Poll question 'Which of these groups do you feel closest to?' 21 per cent chose 'Americans' and 31 per cent chose 'people in countries like Australia, New Zealand and Canada' but 31 per cent chose 'people on the continent of Europe'.[19] These results were in dramatic contrast with the results of earlier polls.

As Commonwealth ties continued to fray, Britain's pattern of trade kept shifting towards Europe. In the early 1950s only 13 per cent of Britain's exports had gone to the countries which were to form the EEC, but by 2000 59 per cent of British exports crossed the Channel (or rolled underneath it) to EU countries and 49 per cent of British imports came from the EU.[20] Ties to Europe were also strengthened by the fact that ever-greater prosperity made it possible for more and more Britons to spend holidays on the continent. In the 1950s and 1960s relatively few Britons had visited Europe, but by the 1980s this was no longer the case. Roughly 80 per cent of foreign holidays involved European travel which brought millions of Britons into direct contact with various facets of European life (see table 13.4).

Table 13.4 *Foreign holidays taken by British residents, 1951–2000*

1951	1961	1971	1981	1991	2000
1,500,000	4,000,000	4,201,000	13,131,000	20,788,000	36,700,000

Sources: Social Trends 1970, Table 33, p. 80; *Social Trends 1973*, Table 38, p. 97; *Social Trends 2000*, Table 13.15, p. 217.

The growth of pro-European sentiment was also supported by the increasing size of the middle class, already discussed in Chapter 2. British opinion about EEC membership had always been divided along class lines. Education and affluence had consistently been associated with pro-European views, professional, managerial and administrative workers being far more likely to support membership than manual workers, and this helps to explain why the Labour Party only became predominantly pro-European in the late 1980s.

These trends encouraged the growth of pro-European sentiment, but during the 1990s their influence was to be counter-balanced by mounting concerns about potential loss of legal and financial sovereignty. The EEC became the EC in 1991 and the European Union in 1993. During the 1990s the steadily-increasing likelihood that EU members would establish a single currency served to focus the anxieties of British Eurosceptics. Economic and Monetary Union and the single interest rate which it entailed implied an inevitable loss of financial sovereignty. As amended, the Treaty of Maastricht of 1992 gave Britain the right to opt out of joining EMU and this served to increase uncertainty as to what some future government would decide and thus made EMU a natural subject for heated debate. The case for participation in European financial affairs was hardly helped by Britain's being forced to remove sterling from the Exchange Rate Mechanism on 16 September 1992, a humiliating experience which suggested that participation in European currency alignments did not guarantee a certain outcome.

Under these circumstances, British public opinion changed course yet again. According to *Eurobarometer*, by spring 2000 only 25 per cent of Britons believed that Britain benefited from EU membership, the lowest level of support of any member nation.[21] Similarly, only 22 per cent of Britons favoured the euro replacing the pound, with the result that Britain had the lowest level of euro support of any EU country.[22] Moreover, whereas belief that EEC/EU membership was a good thing had stood at 57 per cent in 1991, by spring 2000 it had dropped to just 25 per cent. Yet the fact that 51 per cent of Britons believed that membership was neither good nor bad or else had no opinion suggested not so much a surge of anti-European feeling as sheer puzzlement at the complex issues posed by the growth of European institutions.[23]

Euroscepticism was evoked by more than one issue. For one thing, the EU was split by a geographic, cultural and religious divide between industrialised northern European countries which were net contributors to the Union's finances and their poorer southern neighbours which were net recipients. Germany, the UK, the Netherlands and Scandinavia were all net contributors, whereas Greece, Italy, Spain, Portugal and Ireland were all net recipients. It was hardly coincidental that the citizens of the recipient nations were strong supporters of the EU whereas the citizens of the net contributors were considerably less enthusiastic.[24] Scepticism was also evoked by the fact that it was not possible to know how well a single interest rate would serve a continent with many languages and a largely immobile workforce. It was all very well to cite American precedents, but Americans were highly mobile, most of them spoke the same language, and vast numbers of those who had migrated to seek a better life (such as the millions of blacks who left the deep south in the 1930s and 1940s) had endured levels of discrimination and deprivation which would be unacceptable in late twentieth-century Europe. If a uniform interest rate caused high unemployment in Europe's poorer nations, would wealthy nations do an adequate job of helping their poorer neighbours? And how well would EMU cope with a major recession?

In psychological terms, potential loss of Britain's economic sovereignty evoked deep-seated tribal fears. From the Armada to the Battle of Britain, some of the greatest turning points of Britain's past had involved repelling the threat of domination by European powers. EMU could be seen as opening the door to the very domination against which Britons had always fought. Such perceptions fed on atavistic and chauvinistic instincts, but history could not easily be ignored. The governance of major continental nations had a chequered past, and no one could know who might wield power in decades let alone centuries to come.

Such concerns could hardly be taken lightly, but there were also strong arguments in favour of joining the monetary union. From its very origins what became the European Union had represented a profoundly determined effort by Europeans to awake from the nightmare of their own past. The results had been so successful that by the late 1990s war between France and Germany had become unimaginable. Moreover, the single currency inaugurated on 1 January 1999 might well produce far more efficient European markets and a rationalisation of European production, as national markets were subsumed within the larger whole made up of 290 million potential consumers. If Britain remained aloof it could hardly expect to play much of a role in shaping interest and exchange rates and budgetary policies relating to this vast market. Moreover, refusal to join might lead to a curtailment of foreign investment in British manufacturing, and exports to the continent – Britain's largest overseas market – might suffer. It was true that joining EMU would decrease Britain's economic autonomy, but that might be a price worth paying if Britain's long-term economic self-interest would be well served. EMU offered no guarantees, but what was the alternative? Arguably the greatest weakness of the Eurosceptic case was the failure to present a viable alternative.

Given the strength of both sides of the argument, it was hardly surprising that British public opinion continued to resemble an ultra-slow-motion version of a cat twitching its tail, torn by conflicting emotions which it could not resolve and unable to make a lasting decision. Fortunately, no such decision was yet called for because the first Blair government had promised to hold a national referendum prior to any decision to join EMU and had made it clear that such a step would not be taken before a second term in office. Anyway, it was far from clear that a referendum – whatever the result – would signify the end of the highly unstable character of British public opinion regarding the European Union and its institutions. After all, the ambivalence which gave rise to that instability had deep historical roots.

At bottom what was involved was not just economic sovereignty but national identity. At the end of the twentieth century it was still by no means clear that ever greater involvement in European institutions was compatible with Britons' collective sense of themselves.

According to research carried out in 1997, in comparison with Germans, Swedes and Spaniards a far higher proportion of Britons took pride in their nation's past. Moreover, Britons had a particularly strong sense of the continuity between past and present.[25] In addition, 45 per cent of all Britons believed that 'in a united Europe, the various nations will lose their culture and individuality'.[26] Given such sentiments it was unlikely that Britons would suddenly redefine themselves as fully-fledged Europeans, nor were they likely to favour joining EMU unless they were persuaded that Britain's long-term interests would not be damaged irrevocably by the loss of economic sovereignty which joining would entail. As the twentieth century came to an end, public opinion remained so strongly against joining EMU that it was far from clear what the future would bring.

Conclusion

In analysing the profound changes in British life which took place between 1950 and 2000, three main themes have emerged. First, the unparalleled rise in standards of living made it possible for most Britons to live in ways which would have been far beyond their parents' means fifty years earlier. Second, there was a marked decline in popular support for orthodox institutions such as the police, the monarchy, religion, marriage and the trade unions. Third, British society became far more flexible and diverse than it had been in 1950. These three trends interacted at many different levels and in many different ways.

Probably the most important interaction involved the extent to which the rise in standards of living as well as the decline of support for old orthodoxies made possible a freer and more diverse society. Higher standards of living gave Britons a plethora of choices: they ate a wider variety of food than ever before, owned cars as never before and visited far-away places as never before. All manner of information entered British homes as a result of telephones, television and the internet. At a more mundane level, the do-it-yourself store and emulsion paint (both post-war innovations) made it easy for Britons to redecorate their houses in a wide variety of colours, and by the end of the 1990s stirring tales of interior make-overs had become prime-time television fare.

Diversity and choice were also made possible by the decline of support for long-established institutions. The decline of support for the monarchy (as opposed to admiration for the Queen herself) reflected a decreasing respect for inherited status which found practical expression in the decision to end the dominance of hereditary peers in the House of Lords. As to religion, one by-product of the decline of Christian observance was the widespread opening of retail businesses on Sunday and the conversion of Sunday into a day devoted to sociability, shopping and household chores.[1]

The decline of belief in Christianity also contributed to the decline of respect for marriage. Marriage ceased to be sacrosanct in an age when sex began over a decade before nuptial vows, 39 per cent of all babies were born out of wedlock and half of all marriages ended in divorce. The nature of marriage was also affected by the decline of the belief that wives and mothers should not seek employment, and after about 1970 far more career opportunities became available to women with qualifications and university degrees.

Before the 1950s relatively few Britons enjoyed the benefits of higher education and most of those Britons were male and white. By 2000, there were ten times as many students in higher education as there had been in 1954. Moreover, there were more female than male students and the proportion of students who were members of ethnic minorities was larger than the proportion of Britons who belonged to those minorities. Not only were British students more diverse, they also studied a wider variety of subjects including newly-popular topics such as management and computing. By the end of the twentieth century, greatly-increased numbers of students and the expanded role of higher education made it a far more important determinant of social class than ever before.

The decline of faith in old orthodoxies also affected politics. The new-found pragmatism of the Blair era made it possible for the Labour Party to shed its socialist skin. Moreover, the decline of allegiance to a different set of political verities led to an identity crisis within the Conservative Party, which found itself speaking for a shrinking and increasingly elderly segment of the population. Both of the major political parties found that long cherished values had lost much of their resonance as far as the electorate was concerned.

By the late 1950s youth too had begun to define itself in new terms, and youthful consumers of music, clothing and food began to provide a vibrant new market which had not existed before the war. During the course of the 1960s youth established a new identity rooted in radical politics, and although that radicalism disappeared during the Thatcher era the youthful consumer was here to stay. By 2000 youth lasted longer than it had in 1950 partly because more years were spent in education and marriage took place at a later age. The prolongation of youth also stemmed from later entry to full-time employment, a development which did not serve the interests of young working-class males with limited education and few marketable skills.

On a very different note, the final section of this book explored the ways in which three developments of external origin redefined many aspects of British life. Between 1950 and 2000, British architecture went through two major transitions. During the 1950s, British architects rejected insularity in favour of international modernism, yet the hegemony of the international style lasted for only about twenty years. By the 1970s British architects had begun to work in new styles derived from modernism, and the most talented architects went on to design large buildings of singular originality. On the other hand, most new housing remained conservative and unimaginative.

A second factor of external origin, American culture, also had a pervasive impact on British life. American cultural influence took so many forms that it would be impossible to summarise the results in a few sentences. American influence certainly led to more colourful clothing, particularly leisure wear, a host of new foods, and longer opening hours as British stores and restaurants followed American practices and stayed open during the evening and on Sunday. Just as the supermarket (including its trolleys) had been a transatlantic import, so motorway restaurants were modelled on American examples. Moreover, a host of Americanisms entered British speech, as transport gave way to transportation and nothing was over till the fat lady sang.

The third external factor which affected British life was Britain's changing relationship with Europe. In 1962 Dean Acheson said that 'Great Britain has lost an empire and has not yet found a role.'[2]

Britain's loss of empire was eventually followed by membership of the European Community, but by the end of the twentieth century Britons had still not decided to what extent their national identity should be defined by a European future. Nevertheless, almost thirty years of membership of what had become the European Union as well as factors such as modern transport and communication had led to Britons' relationship with Europe becoming far more intimate than it had once been. The Channel Tunnel was here to stay as was the newly-popular continental holiday, and whether Britain eventually joined the European Monetary Union or not, things would never be the same again.

Taken as a whole, the history of British life between 1950 and 2000 can be seen as a tale of progress. Yet it would be inappropriate to end on a Whiggish note. For one thing, the fruits of prosperity were not shared equally and the poor lost out. Moreover, drugs and crime became much more serious problems than they had been in less prosperous times. As to the economy, private prosperity depended

12 The Millenium Dome, London (Richard Rogers and Partners, 1997)

on taxation of private wealth at levels acceptable to middle England and this led to the public sector being starved of funds. By 2000 the National Health Service, schools, universities and the rail network had all been seriously under-funded for so many decades that how or when their deep-rooted problems were going to be solved was far from clear. Finally, while the decline of aesthetic and spiritual orthodoxy had many benefits it did not always lead to satisfactory results, as the saga of the Millennium Dome so clearly demonstrated.

Britons were not sure how to view the millennium. The year 2000 could have been celebrated in a purely religious way, but that would have lacked broad popular appeal in post-religious Britain.

13 Tate Modern, London (Herzog and de Meuron, 2000). The immense Turbine Hall

14 The London Eye
(Marks Barfield, 2000)

In search of the monumental, the government decided to pay for large structures such as the imaginative Millennium Bridge across the Tyne at Newcastle. The most highly publicised of these structures was, however, the Millennium Dome, designed by Sir Richard Rogers and built near London at Greenwich. There was nothing wrong with the Dome itself; the problem was what to put in it. The millennium was not an inherently British occasion, so the great and the good found it difficult indeed to decide what should go inside Rogers' elegant shell. After endless consultation and some false starts the Dome's contents were designed to offend no one. The result was predictably anodyne, and attendance fell far below predictions. Egged on by the tabloids, a sceptical public eventually came to the conclusion that it would have been better to have spent the money on hospitals. Unfortunately, the Dome could not be turned into a hospital. The Dome swallowed more and more public money and finally went bust in the autumn of 2000. All in all, there was something slightly biblical about the tale. Perhaps the moral was that abandoning old loyalties may produce spaces which are hard to fill.

In contrast, both Tate Modern and the London Eye proved to be a great success. Tate Modern involved remodelling a huge old power plant on the south bank of the Thames to take maximum advantage of its immense interior space and provide a home for the most important collection of modern art in the United Kingdom. The result was exciting and the new museum proved to be popular indeed. Also sited on the south bank of the Thames, the London Eye was just plain fun. Essentially a giant Ferris wheel, the Eye stood within full view of the mother of parliaments, and the juxtaposition of the two made some Britons uncomfortable. Yet that juxtaposition was perhaps not a bad symbol of how things stood at the end of the century.

Notes

Abbreviations

The following abbreviations have been used in the notes and bibliography:

CSO: Central Statistical Office
DEE: Department of Education and Employment
DEFRA: Department for Environment, Food and Rural Affairs
DETR: Department of the Environment, Transport and the Regions
HMSO: Her Majesty's Stationery Office
NIACE: National Institute for Adult Continuing Education
ONS: Office for National Statistics
SO: Stationery Office

Preface

1 A. Marwick, *British Society Since 1945* (London: Penguin, 1996), p. 12.
2 E. Royle, 'Trends in Post-war British Social History' in J. Obelkevich and P. Catterall (eds), *Understanding Post-War British Society* (London: Routledge, 1994), p. 17.
3 *Social Trends 2002* (London: ONS, SO, 2002), Table 1.1, p. 28.

Introduction

1 *Independent*, 25 November 1998.
2 D. Cannadine, *Class in Britain* (New Haven: Yale University Press, 1998), p. 22.
3 *Financial Times*, 3 August 1995.
4 *Dod's Parliamentary Companion 1996* (London: Dod's Publishing, 1996), p. 446.
5 *The Whitehall Companion 1997–98* (London: Dod's Publishing, 1997), pp. 1–332. I have not included the 147 civil servants whose names are listed in the directory but who did not provide information concerning their education.

6 G. Orwell, *The Lion and the Unicorn* (1941) (Harmondsworth: Penguin, 1982), p. 52.

7 A. H. Halsey, *Change in British Society* (Oxford: Oxford University Press, 1995), p. 29.

8 K. Young, 'Class, Race and Opportunity' in *British Social Attitudes, 9th Report* (Aldershot: Dartmouth, 1992), pp. 175–6.

9 E. Jacobs and R. Worcester, *Typically British? The Prudential MORI Guide* (London: Bloomsbury, 1991), p. 119.

10 *Social Trends 2002*, Table 1.11, p. 34.

11 As cited in D. Smith, *North and South* (London: Penguin, 1989), p. 180.

12 I. Reid, *Social Class Differences in Britain* (London: Fontana, 1989), p. 39.

13 Young, 'Class, Race and Opportunity', pp. 177–8 and unpublished data supplied by MORI from a survey completed in 1991 as cited in I. Reid, *Class in Britain* (Cambridge: Polity Press, 1998), p. 37.

14 A. H. Halsey, *Change in British Society*, pp. 12–13.

15 ONS statistics for 1997–99 as cited in *Guardian*, 29 January 2002.

16 Reid, *Class in Britain*, p. 57.

17 *Living in Britain: Results from the 2000 General Household Survey* (London: SO, 2001), Table 7.5, p. 85.

18 *Labour Market Trends* (London: ONS, SO, August 2000), Table C.4, p. S44.

19 *Social Trends 2002*, Table 3.11, p. 59.

20 *Ibid.*, Table 13.1, p. 210 and D. G. Hessayon, *The Rose Expert* (Waltham Cross: PBI Publications, 1988), p. 3.

21 Jacobs and Worcester, *Typically British?* p. 78.

22 National Trust U.K. membership in December 2000 as provided by the National Trust.

23 M. Wiener, *English Culture and the Decline of the Industrial Spirit 1850–1980* (Cambridge: Cambridge University Press, 1981), p. 6.

Chapter 1—In prosperous times

1 B. Supple, 'British Economic Decline Since 1945' in R. Floud and D. McCloskey (eds), *The Economic History of Britain Since 1700, vol. 3, 1939–1992* (Cambridge: Cambridge University Press, 1994), p. 325 and *Social Trends 2001*, p. 80.

2 For example, see R. Brown and D. Julius, 'Is Manufacturing Still Special?' in *The Amex Bank Review*, 15 November 1993, vol. 20, no. 9, pp. 2–3.

3 R. Price and G. S. Bain, 'The Labour Force' in A. H. Halsey (ed.), *British Social Trends Since 1900* (Basingstoke: Macmillan, 1988), p. 174.

4 *Social Trends 1995*, Table 4.25, p. 76 and *Labour Market Trends*, February 2001, p. 75.

5 *Social Trends 2002*, p. 87.

6 *Ibid*, p. 165 and *Regional Trends 36* (London: ONS, SO, 2001), Table 6.4, p. 86.

7 *Regional Trends 36*, 2001, Table 6.4, p. 86 and W. D. Rubinstein, *Capitalism, Culture and Decline in Britain, 1750–1900* (London: Routledge, 1993), Table 1.8, p. 42.

8 *Abstract of Regional Statistics*, no. 3 (London: HMSO, 1967), Table 49, p. 57, *Living in Britain: Preliminary Results from the 1994 General Household Survey* (London: HMSO, 1995), Table A7, p. 17, *Annual Abstract of Statistics, 2002*, Table 8.4, p. 124 and *Family Spending: A Report on the 1998–99 Family Expenditure Survey* (London: ONS, SO, 1999), Table 9.3, p. 144.

9 *Social Trends 2001*, Table 13.2, p. 224 and p. 233.

10 As quoted in A. Marwick, *Britain in the Century of Total War* (London: Bodley Head, 1968), p. 249.

11 *Regional Trends 36*, 2001, Table 8.16, p. 114.

12 *Social Trends 2001*, Table 13.6, p. 227.

13 *Ibid.*, p. 212 and *Social Trends 1998*, pp. 218–19. With regard to numerous changes in the British house and its contents, see J. Obelkevich, 'Consumption' in Obelkevich and Catterall, *Understanding*, pp. 141–54.

14 C. Driver, *The British at Table* (London: Hogarth Press, 1983), pp. 108 and 174.

15 J. Burnett, *Plenty and Want: A Social History of Diet in England from 1815 to the Present Day* (London: Routledge, 1989), p. 243.

16 *Domestic Food Consumption and Expenditure, 1950*, Report of the National Food Survey Committee (1952), p. 49.

17 M. E. Chase, *In England Now* (London: Collins, 1937), pp. 133–4.

18 Driver, *The British*, pp. 38–40 and S. Toland, 'Changes in Living Standards since the 1950s', *Social Trends 1980*, p. 18.

19 E. David, *A Book of Mediterranean Food* (London: Dorling Kindersley, 1950), p. v.

20 *Ibid.*, p. vi.

21 *Ibid.*, (2nd edn, 1958), p. 13.

22 *The Good Food Guide 1951–1952*, (London: Consumer's Association, 1951), p. 19.

23 *Ibid.*, pp. 28–180.

24 C. Peach (ed.), *Ethnicity in the 1991 Census*, vol. 2 (London: HMSO, 1996), p. 9.

25 Driver, *The British*, pp. 77–80 and *Independent on Sunday*, 3 March 1996.

26 *Social Trends 1993*, p. 149 and *Social Trends 2002*, p. 217.

27 Mintel, *1998 British Lifestyles* (London: Mintel International, 1998), Figure 8.3.

28 *Social Trends 1995*, p. 126 and *Datamonitor* as cited in *Independent*, 9 February 2000.

29 *Social Trends*, 1998, p. 114.

30 *Ibid.,1970*, Table 25, p. 70 and *Ibid., 2001*, Table 4.8, p. 78.

31 *Independent on Sunday*, 19 March 1995, *Financial Times*, 22 August 1995 and *Retailing Inquiry/Mintel* as cited in *Independent*, 2 March 1996.

32 *The Times*, 12 February, 1998.

33 *National Food Survey 2000* (London: DEFRA, SO, 2001), p. 36.

34 *Social Trends 2000*, p. 200.

35 *Annual Abstract of Statistics, 2002*, Table 14.11, p. 214.

36 J. Glancey, 'What Are Towns For?', *Independent*, 2 November 1994 and *The Impact of Large Food Stores on Market Towns and District Centres* (London: DETR, 1998), p. 5. The conventional definition of the superstore is that it has over 2,500 square metres of sales floor space.

37 S. McClarence, 'Pleasure Cruises in the British Aisles',*Independent*, 13 November 1994, J. Myerson, 'Mall is Beautiful', *Independent on Sunday*, 15 November 1998 and *Independent*, 15 March 1999.

38 McClarence, 'Pleasure'.

39 Toland, 'Changes,' p. 31 and *Annual Abstract of Statistics 2002*, Table 14.7, p. 211.

40 *Annual Abstract of Statistics 2002*, Tables 14.1, p. 207 and 14.4, p. 209 and *Transport Statistics Great Britain 2000* (London: DETR, SO, 2000), Table 9.1, p. 177.

41 *Transport Trends* (London: DETR, SO, 2001), Table 3.2, p. 37.

42 *Transport Statistics Great Britain 2000*, Table 4.14, p. 97 and *Focus on London 2000* (London: ONS, SO, 2000), Table 10.7, p. 117.

43 *Social Trends 2002*, Table 11.3, p. 182.

44 *Annual Abstract of Statistics 2002*, Table 14.3, p. 208.

45 *Transport Statistics Great Britain 2000*, Table 9.9, p. 185.

Chapter 2—Slicing the pie

1 *Regional Trends 2001*, Table 8.1, p. 107.

2 *Ibid.*, Table 5.3, p. 67.

3 *Ibid.*, p. 131 and Table 6.5, p. 87.

4 *Ibid.*, Table 8.12, p. 112.

5 *Labour Market Trends*, November 2000, Table B.3, p. S22 and Halsey, *Change*, pp. 35 and 99.

6 A. Heath, R. Jowell and J. Curtice, *How Britain Votes* (Oxford: Pergamon, 1985), pp. 35–6. See also A. Heath, *Understanding Political Change* (Oxford: Pergamon, 1991), p. 203.

7 J. Curtice, 'Political Sociology 1945–92' in Obelkevich and Catterall, *Understanding*, p. 35.

8 *Sunday Times*, 1 August 1996 and 1 September 1996.

9 *Households Below Average Income, 1979–1994–95* (London: SO, 1997), Table A.1, p. 116. The homeless and those living in temporary bed and breakfast accommodation were not included in these statistics.

10 J. Lowe, *Giving and Inheriting* (London: Which?, 1994), Table 1.2, p. 11.

11 *Population Trends*, winter 1996, Table 3, p. 17.

12 *Social Focus on the Unemployed* (London: ONS, SO, 1998), p. 59.

13 *Social Trends 2001*, p. 163.

14 *Ibid.* Table 9.3, p. 162.

15 *Home Office Statistical Bulletin*, 24 September 1996, *The 1996 British Crime Survey*, England and Wales, p. 25.

16 *Social Trends 2002*, pp. 150 and 154.

17 H. S. Commager, 'English Traits, One Hundred Years Later', *The Nineteenth Century*, July 1948, as reprinted in H. S. Commager (ed.), *Britain Through American Eyes* (London: Bodley Head, 1974), pp. 751–2.

18 G. Gorer, *Exploring English Character* (London: Cresset Press, 1955), p. 213.

19 Home Office Research and Statistics Directorate, *Research Findings No. 60*, C. Mirrlees-Black and T. Budd, 'Policing and the Public: Findings From the 1996 *British Crime Survey*', pp. 1–2.

20 R. Tarling and L. Dowds, 'Crime and Punishment' in *British Social Attitudes, 14th Report, 1997–98*, p. 205.

21 *Home Office Statistical Bulletin*, 21 September 2000, 'Police Complaints and Discipline' (London: ONS, 2000), pp. 6–7 and 10.

Chapter 3—The monarchy and the aristocracy

1 L. Harris, *Long to Reign Over Us? The Status of the Royal Family in the Sixties* (London: Kimber, 1966), p. 75.

2 *Sunday Times*, 14 February 1993 and J. Dimbleby, *The Prince of Wales* (London: Little Brown, 1994), p. 552.

3 D. Cannadine, 'The British Monarchy and the Invention of Tradition' in E. Hobsbawm and T. Ranger (eds), *The Invention of Tradition* (Cambridge: Cambridge University Press, 1983), pp. 24 and 137.

4 D. Tomlinson, *Divine Right: The Inglorious Survival of the British Royalty* (London: Abacus, 1995), pp. 213–17.

5 Prince Charles to C. Fellowes, 23 October 1992, as quoted in Dimbleby, *Prince*, p. 501.

6 *The Times*, 27 August 1998

7 V. Bogdanor, *The Monarchy and the Constitution* (Oxford: Clarendon Press. 1995), p. 305.

8 R. McKibbin, *Classes and Cultures England 1918–1951* (Oxford: Oxford University Press, 1998), pp. 4 and 6.

9 *Independent*, 20 August 1996 and *Financial Times*, 20 August 1996.

10 *Independent*, 20 April 1996.

Chapter 4—Religion

1 J. Dimbleby, conversation with Prince Charles, Dimbleby, *Prince*, p. 246.

2 *Independent on Sunday*, 17 January 1999.

3 P. Brierley, *A Century of British Christianity: Historical Statistics 1900–1985* (Bromley: Marc Europe, 1989) and *Social Trends 1999*, Table 13.23, p. 220.

4 C. G. Brown, *The Death of Christian Britain* (London: Routledge, 2001), Table 8.1, p. 191.

5 S. Bruce, *Religion in Modern Britain* (Oxford: Oxford University Press, 1995), pp. 13, 32–3 and 35 and *Financial Times*, 8 May 1997.

6 *Social Trends 1999*, Table 13.23, p. 220.

7 *Ibid.*, Table 13.22, p. 220 and *Social Trends 2001*, Table 13.23, p. 235.

8 J. White, 'Death of the British Sunday', *Independent*, 14 December 1994.

9 *Social Trends 1999*, Table 13.23, p. 220.

10 *Social Focus on Women* (London: HMSO, 1995), p. 15.

11 S. Bruce and F. Alderdice, 'Religious Belief and Behaviour' in *Social Attitudes in Northern Ireland* (Belfast: Blackstaff, 1993), p. 7.

12 *Ibid.*, p. 8.

13 K. Trew, 'National Identity' in *Social Attitudes in Northern Ireland* (Belfast: Blackstaff, 1996), Table 1, p. 142.

Chapter 5—Marriage

1 K. Wellings, J. Field, A. M. Johnson and J. Wadsworth, *Sexual Behaviour in Britain* (London: Penguin, 1994), p. 248.

2 *Population Trends 1*, autumn 1975 (London: Office of Population Censuses and Surveys) Table 16, p. 35 and *Population Trends 107*, spring 2002, Table 1.6, p. 62.

3 *Social Trends 2001*, Table 2.2, p. 42 and *Living in Britain: General Household Survey 2000*, p. 10.

4 K. Wellings *et al.*, 'Sexual Behaviour in Britain: Early Heterosexual Experience' *The Lancet*, 1 December 2001, p. 1846.

5 *Social Trends 1999*, Table 2.13, p. 48 and *Population Trends 103*, spring 2001, Table 9.1, p. 79.

6 Wellings *et al.*, 'Sexual Behaviour', p. 71.

7 P. Larkin, 'Annus Mirabilis,' *High Windows* (London: Faber and Faber, 1974), p. 34.

8 Wellings *et al.*, 'Sexual Behaviour', p. 48.

9 *Social Trends 2000*, Table 2.19, p. 45.

10 *Social Trends 1997*, Table 2.26, p. 52, *Abortion Statistics*, series AB, no. 24 (London: ONS, 1997), p. 3 and telephone call to Information Statistics Division, Scotland, 25 August 1999.

11 *Social Trends 1971*, Table 84, p. 120 and *Annual Abstract of Statistics 2001*, Table 6.8, p. 73.

12 P. Summerfield, 'Women in Britain since 1945' in Obelkevich and Catterall, *Understanding*, p. 62 and *Social Trends 2001*, Table 4.2, p. 75.

13 *Population Trends 95*, spring 1999, Table 1, p. 61 and *Annual Abstract of Statistics, 2002*, Table 5.12, p. 42.

14 *Social Trends 1999*, p. 49.

15 *Population Trends 107*, spring 2002, Table 1.6, p. 62.

16 *Social Trends 2002*, Chart A1, p. 18.

17 *Social Trends 1994*, Table 2.22, p. 40, *Population Trends 103*, spring 2001, Tables 3.1 and 3.2, pp. 68–9 and findings of the Institute for Social and Economic Research of the University of Essex as cited in *Independent*, 22 November 2000.

18 *Social Focus on the Unemployed*, p. 13.

19 *Independent*, 11 December 1997.

20 *Population Trends 103*, spring 2001, Table 3.3, p. 70.

21 *Labour Market Trends*, February 2001, p. 111.

Chapter 6—The trade unions

1 *Social Trends 1995*, Table 4.21, p. 74 and *Labour Market Trends*, May 2001, Table 5, p. 238.

2 *Social Trends 1996*, p. 92.

3 *Labour Party Seventeenth Annual Report* (1918), p. 140 as quoted in H. Pelling and A. J. Reid, *A Short History of the Labour Party* (11th edn) (Basingstoke: Macmillan, 1996), p. 39.

4 R. Price and G. S. Bain, 'The Labour Force' in Halsey (ed.), *British Social Trends*, Table 4.13, pp. 195–6.

5 J. Callaghan, *Time and Chance* (London: Collins, 1987), p. 537.

6 R. Taylor, *The Trade Union Question in British Politics* (Oxford: Blackwell, 1993), p. 275.

7 *Ibid.*, p. 297 and E. Hopkins, *The Rise and Decline of the English Working Classes 1918–1990* (London: Weidenfield and Nicolson, 1991), p. 226.

8 As quoted in Pelling and Reid, *A Short History*, pp. 39 and 191.

Chapter 7—Education

1 Ministry of Education, 'Maintained and Assisted Primary and Secondary Schools', *Stats, Return*, No. 8, January 1955, pp. 3 and 7.

2 'Comprehensive Education: Reorganisation of City Secondary Schools', Report of the Director of Education, City of Liverpool Education Committee, 1964, as quoted in B. Simon, *Education and the Social Order, 1940–1990* (London: Lawrence and Wishart, 1991), p. 272.

3 DES, *Statistics of Education, 1975 Schools*, vol. 1, London, 1975, p. x and Table 1.

4 J. Paxman, *Friends in High Places: Who Runs Britain?* (London: Penguin, 1990), p. 164.

5 See P. H. Hirst, 'The Foundations of the National Curriculum: Why Subjects?' in P. O'Hear and J. White, *Assessing the National Curriculum* (London: Paul Chapman, 1993), pp. 31–7.

6 S. Jenkins, *Accountable to None* (London: Hamish Hamilton, 1995), pp. 119–21.

7 *Independent*, 20 June 1996 and 10 April 1997.

8 *Social Trends 2001*, Table 3.1, p. 58.

9 ICM poll cited in *Guardian*, 7 February 1996.

10 *Financial Times*, 3 October, 1998.

11 Rubinstein, *Capitalism, Culture and Decline*, pp. 113 and 119.

12 Winchester College, 'Notions' (pamphlet), Winchester, n.d., pp. 20–5.

13 G. Walford, *Life in Public Schools* (London: Methuen, 1986), Table 1.2, p. 13.

14 *Ibid*, p. 238.

15 *Ibid.*, p. 5, *Social Trends 1995*, Table 3.10, p. 50, *Social Trends 2000*, Table 3.2, p. 50 and *ISIS, Annual Census 2000*, p. 6.

16 *Statistics of Education Schools in England 2000* (London: SO, 2000), Table 44, p. 70 and Table 48, p. 73.

17 *Independent*, 24 April 2002.

18 *ISIS, Annual Census 2001*, Table J, p. 23.

19 *Ibid.*, p. 11.

20 *Social Trends 1970*, Table 85, p. 132, *Annual Abstract of Statistics 2001*, Table 6.8, p. 73 and A. H. Halsey, 'Further and Higher Education', Table 6.2, p. 225 in A. H. Halsey and J. Webb, *Twentieth-Century British Social Trends* (Basingstoke: Macmillan, 2000).

21 Simon, *Education*, p. 223.

22 *Higher Education, Report of the Committee Appointed by the Prime Minister Under the Chairmanship of Lord Robbins 1961–1963*, Cmnd 2154 (London: HMSO, 1963), pp. 51 and 66.

23 *Ibid.*, pp. 8, 67–70 and 277.

24 *Ibid.*, pp. 196–7, 281, 284–5, and 287.

25 R. Lazard, J. King and C. Morse, *The Impact of Robbins* (Harmondsworth: Penguin, 1969), Table 2, p. 23.

26 *Higher Education Funding Council, Annual Report 1994–95*, Bristol, 1995, p. 13

27 D. Blunkett, 'The Tough Truths of Dearing', *The Times*, 24 July 1997.

28 *Independent*, 22 June 1995 and 24 June 1998, K. S. Davies, P. Walker and D. Tupman, 'Universities, Numbers, Money, and Policies, 1945–85' in W. A. C. Stewart, *Higher Education in Postwar Britain* (Basingstoke: Macmillan, 1989), Table 15.14, p. 285 and *Higher Education Funding Council, Annual Report 1994–95*, pp. 4 and 13.

29 *Social Trends 1996*, Table 3.28, p. 79.

30 R. Crompton, 'Where Did All the Bright Girls Go? Women's Higher Education and Employment Since 1964' in N. Abercrombie and A. Warde, *Social Change in Contemporary Britain* (Cambridge: Polity Press, 1992), pp. 57–9.

31 P. Taylor, 'Access to Higher Education: An Uneven Path?' in H. Goulbourne and P. Lewis-Meeks (eds), *Access of Ethnic Minorities to Higher Education in Britain*, Centre for Research in Ethnic Relations, Occasional Paper in Ethnic Relations no. 10, Warwick, 1993, pp. 6–11 and T. Modood, 'The Number of Ethnic Minority Students in British Higher Education: Some Grounds for Optimism', *Oxford Review of Education*, vol. 9, no. 2 (1993), pp. 177–8.

Chapter 8—Ethnic minorities

1 C. Peach (ed.), *Ethnicity in the 1991 Census* (London: HMSO, 1996), vol. 2, p. 5.

2 D. Mason, *Race and Ethnicity in Modern Britain* (Oxford: Oxford University Press, 1995), pp. 22 and 25.

3 Peach, *Ethnicity*, vol. 2, Tables 4–5, pp. 8–9 and *Population Trends*, autumn 2001, Table 1, p. 9. .

4 Peach, *Ethnicity*, vol. 2, p. 9 and J. Eade, T. Vamplew and C. Peach, 'The Bangladeshis: The Encapsulated Community' in Peach, *Ethnicity*, vol. 2, p. 151.

5 Mason, *Race*, p. 24.

6 R. Ballard (ed.), Introduction to *Desh Pardesh: the South Asian Presence in Britain* (London: Hurst, 1994), p. 11.

7 *Population Trends*, autumn 2001, pp. 8–10.

8 R. Ballard, 'Differentiation and Disjunction Among the Sikhs' in Ballard (ed.), *Desh Pardesh*, p. 100.

9 *Labour Market Trends*, January 2001, Table 2, p. 31.

10 *Social Trends 2002*, Table 4.21, p. 81.

11 *Social Focus on Ethnic Minorities* (London: HMSO, 1996), Table 1.6, p. 13.

12 *Ibid*, Table 2.17, p. 28, Table 4.20, p. 49 and Tables 4.22 and 4.23, p. 50, T. Modood, 'Qualifications and English Language' in T. Modood and R. Berthoud (eds), *Ethnic Minorities in Britain* (London: Policy Studies Institute, 1997), p. 79, *Social Trends 1997*, Table 10.5, p. 171 and *Independent*, 22 November 1999.

13 Research by Professor David McEvoy as cited in *Independent*, 5 January 2002.

14 Ballard, Introduction to *Desh Pardesh*, p. 34.

15 *Social Focus on Ethnic Minorities*, p. 15. and K. Gardner and A. Shukar, 'I'm Bengali, I'm Asian and I'm Living Here' in Ballard, *Desh Pardesh*, p. 158.

16 P. Lewis, 'Being Muslim and Being British' in Ballard, *Desh Pardesh*, pp. 79–80.

17 T. Modood, 'Qualifications' Table 3.2, p. 61.

18 A. Berrington, 'Marriage Patterns and Inter-ethnic Unions' in D. Coleman and J. Salt (eds), *Ethnicity in the 1991 Census*, vol. 1 (London: HMSO, 1996), p. 199.

19 Coleman and Salt, *Ethnicity*, vol. 1, Table 7.2, p. 182 and Table 7.3, p. 185.

20 *Labour Market Trends*, March 2001, p. 141.

21 *Social Focus on Ethnic Minorities*, Table 5.18, p. 62.

22 P. Vallely and A. Brown, 'The Best Place to Be a Muslim', *Independent*, 6 December 1995.

23 See Peach, *Ethnicity*, vol. 2, p. 42.

24 K. Young, 'Class, Race and Opportunity' in *British Social Attitudes* (1992), p. 181.

25 A. Adonis and S. Pollard, *A Class Act* (London: Hamish Hamilton, 1997), pp. 249–50.
26 *Social Trends 2002*, Table 9.24, p. 162.

Chapter 9—Women and work

1 P. Summerfield, 'Women in Britain since 1945: Companionate Marriage and the Double Burden' in Obelkevich and Catterall, *Understanding*, p. 62.
2 J. Lewis, *Women in Britain Since 1945* (Oxford: Blackwell, 1992), p. 59.
3 The *Beveridge Report* as cited in K. Hinds and L. Jarvis, 'The Gender Gap' in *British Social Attitudes, 2000–2001*, p. 101.
4 Summerfield, 'Women', pp. 62–3 and B. J. Elliott, 'Demographic Trends in Domestic Life 1945–87', in D. Clark (ed.), *Marriage, Domestic Life and Social Change* (London: Routledge, 1991), p. 102.
5 *Social Focus on Women*, (London: HMSO, 1995) p. 28.
6 *Labour Market Trends*, May 2000, Table 3, p. 191, S. Harkness, 'The Gender Earnings Gap: Evidence from the U.K.' *Fiscal Studies*, vol. 17, no. 2, 1996 and *Social Trends 2002*, p. 70.
7 S. Nickell, 'Unemployment in Britain' in P. Gregg and J. Wadsworth, *The State of Working Britain* (Manchester: Manchester University Press, 1999), Table 1.3, p. 15.
8 *Labour Market Trends*, March 1997, Table 4, p. 108, December 1998, pp. 624–5 and March 2001, pp. 145 and 147.
9 *Labour Market Trends*, February 2001, Table 5, p. 117.
10 *Ibid.*, p. 32 and P. Thane, 'Women Since 1945' in P. Johnson (ed.), *Twentieth-Century Britain* (London: Longman, 1994), p. 395.
11 *Social Focus on Women and Men* (London: ONS, 1998), p. 73.
12 T. Desai, P. Gregg, J. Steer and J. Wadsworth, 'Gender and the Labour Market' in Greg and Wadsworth, *The State*, pp. 175–6 and *Social Trends 2001*, Table 9.24, p. 173.
13 *The 2002 Female FTSE Report*, Cranfield University School of Management, as cited in *Independent on Sunday*, 10 November 2002.
14 *Social Focus on Women and Men*, p. 32.

Chapter 10—Youth and age

1 S. Frith, *The Sociology of Youth* (Ormskirk: Causeway Books, 1984), pp. 2–3 and J. Pilcher, *Age and Gender in Modern Britain* (Oxford: Oxford University Press, 1995), pp. 58 and 72–3.

2 J. R. Gillis, *Youth and History* (London: Academic Press, 1981), pp. 6–7.

3 Wellings *et al.*, 'Sexual Behaviour', pp. 37–8, *Social Trends 1999*, Table 2.13, p. 48 and *Population Trends 103*, Spring 2001, Table 9.1, p. 79.

4 P. Robinson, 'Education, Training and the Youth Labour Market' in Gregg and Wadsworth, *The State*, Table 9.3, p. 152.

5 G. Jones and C. Wallace, *Youth, Family and Citizenship* (Buckingham: Open University Press, 1992), p. 25, *Social Focus on the Unemployed*, p. 28 and *Social Trends 2001*, Table 3.12, p. 64.

6 *Labour Market Trends*, May 2000, Table 1, p. 189 and *Social Trends 1998*, pp. 69 and 73.

7 For a more detailed examination of changes in the transition from school to work, see K. Roberts, *Youth and Unemployment in Modern Britain* (Oxford: Oxford University Press, 1995).

8 M. Abrams, *The Teenage Consumer* (London: 1959–61), p. 5.

9 *Ibid.*, editorial introduction, p. 3.

10 *Ibid.*, pp. 7–9.

11 *Ibid.*, Table 1, 'Expenditure by Teenagers, 1957', p. 10.

12 G. Melly, *Revolt into Style* (London: Allen Lane, 1970), p. 80.

13 *Ibid*, p. 88.

14 J. Weeks, *Coming Out* (London: Quartet Books, 1990), p. 158.

15 *Ibid.*, p. 166.

16 *Gay News*, no. 83, London, 20 November–3 December, 1975, pp. 1–2.

17 Weeks, *Coming Out*, p. 241.

18 S. Harding, 'Trends in Permissiveness' in R. Jowell *et al.*, *British Social Attitudes 5th Report*, 1988 (Aldershot: Dartmouth Press, 1992), p. 36.

19 L. Brook, 'The Public's Response to AIDS' in R. Jowell *et al.*, *British Social Attitudes 5th Report, 1988*, p. 74.

20 For evidence of this change in attitude see K. Hinds and L. Jarvis, 'The Gender Gap' in *British Social Attitudes 17th Report*, 2000–2001, p. 112.

21 For a thoughtful discussion of the emergence of Soho as a centre for gay life in the late 1980s and 1990s see F. Mort, *Cultures of Consumption* (London: Routledge, 1996), pp. 149–70.

22 I have used the imprecise phrase 'practicing homosexual' in order to make a distinction between those men and women who have had a homosexual experience at some time in their lives as opposed to the smaller proportion of individuals who have had a homosexual partner within the previous five years. As Wellings, Field, Johnson and Wadsworth have observed, 'the difference between lifetime and current homosexual experience points to the likelihood that homosexual expe-

rience is often a relatively isolated or passing event', Thus, 5 to 6 per cent of British men and 3 per cent of British women have had a homosexual experience at some time in their lives (Wellings *et al.*, 'Sexual Behaviour', pp. 186–203). On the other hand, according to more recent research under the same auspices, only 2.6 per cent of British men and women had homosexual partners within the five years ending in 2001 (A. M. Johnson *et al.*, 'Sexual Behaviour in Britain: Partnerships, Practices and HIV Risk Behaviours', *The Lancet*, 1 December 2001, p. 1839).

23 A. Heath and A. Park, 'Thatcher's Children?' in *British Social Attitudes, 14th Report*, 1997–98, p. 9.

24 P. Thane, *Old Age in English History* (Oxford: Oxford University Press, 2000), p. 386. See also Pilcher, *Age*, pp. 83 and 98–116.

25 A. Tinker, 'Old Age and Gerontology' in Obelkevich and Catterall, *Understanding*, p. 76, *Social Focus on Older People* (London: ONS, 1999), Table 1.1, p. 10 and *Annual Abstract of Statistics, 2002*, Table 5.3, p. 28.

26 *Social Trends 2001*, Table 4.5, p. 77.

27 M. Kohli, 'Work and Retirement: A Comparative Perspective' in M. W. Riley, R. L. Kahn and A. Foner (eds), *Age and Structural Lag* (New York: Wiley, 1994), pp. 80 and 86.

28 R. Disney, 'Why Have Older Men Stopped Working?' in Gregg and Wadsworth, *The State*, p. 65.

29 *Living in Britain, Results from the 2000 General Household Survey*, Table 3.12, p. 20.

30 *Monthly Digest of Statistics*, March 2001, Table 2.2, p. 30.

31 *Social Trends 1999*, Table 8.4, p. 137 and *Social Focus on Older People*, Table 4.15, p. 73.

32 *The Carnegie Inquiry Into the Third Age, Final Report, Life, Work and Livelihood in the Third Age* (Dunfermline: Carnegie United Kingdom Trust, 1993), p. iii.

33 *Ibid.*, p. 11.

34 *Ibid.*, p. 5.

35 Riley *et al.*, *Age*, p. 6.

36 P. Laslett, *A Fresh Map of Life* (London: Macmillan, 1996), p. 219.

37 N. Sargant, *The Learning Divide* (Leicester: NIACE, 1997), pp. vii.

38 Laslett, *Fresh*, p. 213.

39 P. Thompson, C. Itzin and M. Abendstern, *I Don't Feel Old* (Oxford: Oxford University Press, 1990), p. 146.

40 *Ibid.*, p. 143.

41 B. Hayward, S. Taylor, N. Smith and G. Davies, *Evaluation of the Campaign for Older Workers* (London: DEE, 1997), p. 28.

Chapter 11—The new architecture

1 A. Saint, *Towards a Social Architecture* (New Haven: Yale University Press, 1987), p. 1.

2 *Ibid.,* p. 2.

3 R. Blomfield, 'Is Modern Architecture on the Right Track?', a symposium, *The Listener*, 10, 1933, p. 124, as cited in A. Jackson, *The Politics of Architecture* (London: Architectural Publishers, 1970), p. 15.

4 *Ibid.,* pp. 175–6.

5 R. Hewison, *The Heritage Industry* (London: Methuen, 1987), p. 36.

6 Jackson, *The Politics*, p. 166.

7 M. Glendenning and S. Muthesius, *Tower Block* (New Haven: Yale University Press, 1994), p. 1.

8 *Ibid.* and E. Hopkins, *Rise and Decline*, pp. 141–2.

9 Hewison, *Heritage*, p. 37.

10 P. Nuttgens, *The Home Front* (London: BBC, 1989), p. 86 and 1985 study by South Bank Polytechnic cited in *Housing*, February 1994.

11 D. Sudjic, *The Architecture of Richard Rogers* (London: Fourth Estate and Wordsearch, 1994), p. 20.

12 Brick and breeze-block are highly undesirable building materials in earthquake country, where structures must be able to bend like an aircraft wing. The popularity of wood-frame construction in California is by no means an accident.

13 HRH the Prince of Wales, speech to celebrate the 150th anniversary of the Royal Institute of British Architects, 30 May 1984, as quoted in Dimbleby, *Prince*, p. 316.

14 HRH the Prince of Wales, *A Vision of Britain* (London: Doubleday, 1989), p. 77.

15 *Ibid.,* pp. 7–9.

16 *Ibid.,* p. 82.

17 R. Samuel, *Theatres of Memory* (London: Verso, 1994), p. 120.

18 A. Derbyshire, 'Building the Welfare State' in B. Goldstein (ed.), *Architecture: Opportunities, Achievements*, a report of the Annual Conference of the Royal Institute of British Architects held at the University of Hull, 14 to 17 July 1976, (London: 1977), p. 29.

19 *Ibid.,* p. 30.

20 *Ibid.*

21 Samuel, *Theatres*, p. 131.

22 C. Jencks, *What Is Post-Modernism?* (London: Academy Editions, 1989), p. 56.

23 R. MacCormac, 'Architecture, History and Narrative', a lecture given at Oxford University Department for Continuing Education, 11 February 1997.

Chapter 12—Living in the American age

1 D. Dimbleby and D. Reynolds, *An Ocean Apart* (London: Hodder and Stoughton, 1988), pp. 101–2.

2 J. B. Priestley, *English Journey* (1934) (London: Heinemann, 1984), p. 24.

3 J. B. Priestley and J. Hawkes, *Journey Down a Rainbow* (London: Reader's Union, 1957), p. vii. With regard to Priestley's views on imported mass culture, see C. Waters, 'J. B. Priestley 1894–1984' in S. Pedersen and P. Mandler (eds), *After the Victorians* (London: Routledge,1994), pp. 210–11.

4 R. Hoggart, *The Uses of Literacy* (London:Transation Publishers, 1957), pp. 203–04.

5 J. Osborne, *Look Back in Anger* (1957) (London: Faber and Faber, 1996), p. 11.

6 F. Williams, *The American Invasion* (London: A. Blond, 1962), p. 11.

7 *Ibid.*, pp. 12–13.

8 *Mass Observation Bulletin*, April 1947, as quoted in H. D. Willcock, 'Public Opinion: Attitudes Towards America and Russia' *The Political Quarterly*, no. 1, vol. 19, London, 1948, p. 68.

9 H. Hopkins, *The New Look* (London: Reader's Union, 1964), p. 109.

10 D. Snowman, *Kissing Cousins* (London:Temple Smith, 1977), p. 300.

11 *Independent*, 17 June 1998.

12 M.Wood, *America in the Movies* (NewYork: Columbia University Press, 1989), p. 193.

13 *Social Trends 1998*, Table 13.22, p. 226 and *Social Trends 2002*, Table 13.13, p. 217.

14 N.Tiratsoo, 'Limits of Americanisation:The United States Productivity Gospel in Britain' in B. Conekin, F. Mort and C. Waters, *Moments of Modernity* (London: Rivers Oram, 1999), p. 105.

15 *Ibid.*, p. 111.

Chapter 13—The ambivalent Europeans

1 R. Jowell and J. Spence, *The Grudging Europeans: A Study of British Attitudes towards the EEC* (London: Social and Community Planning Reserarch, Centre for Sample Surveys, 1975), S. George, *An Awkward*

Partner (Oxford: Oxford University Press, 1990) and D. Gowland and A. Turner, *Reluctant Europeans* (Harlow: Longman, 2000).

2 P. Gerbet, 'La Genese du Plan Schuman' in *Revue Francaise de Science Politique*, vol. 6, no. 3, Paris, July–September 1956, pp. 549–50.

3 Lord Beloff, *Britain and European Union* (Basingstoke: MacMillan, 1996), p. 6.

4 CP (48) 75, 6 March 1948 'European Economic Cooperation' (in CAB 129/25) as cited in R. Edmunds, *Setting the Mould* (Oxford: Clarendon Press, 1986), p. 190.

5 Gowland and Turner, *Reluctant Europeans*, p. 24.

6 *European Unity*, published by the NEC of the Labour party, May 1950, p. 4 as quoted in Gowland and Turner, *Reluctant Europeans*, p. 85.

7 Gallup Report, *British Attitudes towards the Common Market 1957* (London, 1971), n.p.

8 *Ibid.*

9 *Ibid.*

10 *The Times*, 15 January 1963.

11 *Ibid.*

12 Gallup Report, *British Attitudes*, n.p.

13 *Ibid.* and Gowland and Turner, *Reluctant Europeans*, p. 178.

14 M. Collins, 'Who Voted What' in R. Jowell and G. Hoinville (eds), *Britain Into Europe* (London: Croom Helm, 1976), pp. 93–9.

15 Jowell and Spence, *Grudging*, p. 1.

16 B. Hedges, 'The Final Four Years: From Opposition to Endorsement' in Jowell and Hoinville, *Britain Into Europe*, p. 59.

17 A. King, *Britain Says Yes* (Washington: American Enterprise Institute for Public Policy Research, 1977), pp. 95–6.

18 Gowland and Turner, *Reluctant Europeans*, pp. 206–8.

19 Gallup Political Index, report no. 346, June 1989, as cited in Nugent, 'British Public Opinion' in George, *Britain*, p. 193.

20 *Regional Trends 2001*, Table 13.7, p. 171.

21 *Eurobarometer*, no. 53, spring 2000, Figure 2.2b, p. 10.

22 *Ibid.*, Fig. 3.4, p. 46.

23 *Ibid.*, Fig. 2.1b, p. 8.

24 Q. Peel, 'The EU's Real Split', *Financial Times*, 25 February 1999. The issues summarised in this paragraph were discussed with lucidity and grace by Timothy Garton Ash in 'Europe's Endangered Liberal Order,' *Foreign Affairs*, vol. 77, no. 2, March–April 1998.

25 D. McCrone and P. Surridge, 'National Identity and National Pride' in R. Jowell *et al.*, *British and European Social Attitudes, 15th Report, 1998*, p. 9.

26 G. Evans, 'How Britain Views the EU' in Jowell *et al.*, *British and European* p. 184.

Conclusion

1 See C. D. Field, '"The Secularized Sabbath" Revisited: Opinion Polls as Sources for Sunday Observance in Contemporary Britain', *Contemporary British History*, vol. 15, no. 1, London, 2001, pp. 1–20.

2 As quoted in A. Marwick, *Britain in the Century of Total War*, p. 414.

Bibliography

Newspapers

Financial Times
Guardian
Independent
Independent on Sunday
The Times

Periodicals

Abstract of Regional Statistics, no. 3 (London: HMSO, 1967).
Annual Abstract of Statistics, 1994–2002 (London: ONS, SO, 1994–2002).
Cambridge University Reporter, special no. 21, vol. 130, 23 August 2000.
Contemporary British History, vol. 15, no. 1, London, Spring 2001.
Dod's Parliamentary Companion 1996 (Hailsham, East Sussex: Dod's Parliamentary Companion Ltd, 1996).
Education and Training Statistics for the United Kingdom (London: DEE, SO, 2000).
Eurobarometer no. 33, June 1990 to no. 53, spring 2000, Office for Official Publications of the European Communities, Luxembourg.
Family Spending: A report on the 1998–99 Family Expenditure Survey (London: SO, 1999).
Focus on London 2000 (London: ONS, SO, 2000).
Focus on Public Transport Great Britain 1999 Edition (London: DETR, SO, 1999).
Gay News, no. 83, London, 20 November–3 December 1975.
The Good Food Guide 1951–1952 (London: 1951).
Home Office Statistical Bulletin (London: 1996–2000).
Households Below Average Income 1979–94–95 (London: GSS, SO, 1997).
Housing, February 1994.
Independent Schools Information Service, Annual Census 2000 and 2001 (London: 2000 and 2001).
Labour Market Trends (London: ONS, SO, 1996–2001).

Living in Britain: Results from the 1994–2000 General Household Surveys (London: ONS, SO, 1996–2001).

Monthly Digest of Statistics (London: SO, 1999–2001).

National Food Survey 2000 (London: DEFRA, SO, 2001).

Oxford University Gazette, supplement 4 to no. 3396, Oxford, 4 June 1969 and supplement 2 to no. 4556, 2 August 2000.

The Political Quarterly, no. 1, vol. XIX (London: 1948).

Population Trends, autumn 1975 and autumn 1998–autumn 2001 (London: Office of Population Censuses and Surveys, 1975–2001).

Regional Trends 33–7, 1998–2002 (London: ONS, SO, 1998–2002).

Social Attitudes in Northern Ireland, 1992–97 (Belfast: Blackstaff, 1993–98).

Social Trends, 1994–2002 (London: ONS, SO, 1994–2002).

Statistics of Education, 1975 Schools, vol. 1 (London: DES, 1975).

Statistics of Education, Schools in England 2000 (London: DEE, SO, 2000).

Transport Statistics Great Britain 2000 (London: DETR, SO, 2000).

Transport Trends (London: DETR, SO, 2000–1).

The Whitehall Companion 1997–98 (London: Dod's Publishing and Research, 1997).

Reports

Abrams, M., *The Teenage Consumer* (London: London Press Exchange, 1959–61).

Brierley, P., *A Century of British Christianity: Historical Statistics 1900–1985* (Bromley: MARC Europe, 1989).

The 1996 British Crime Survey, Home Office Statistical Bulletin issue 19/96, 24 September 1996.

Coleman, J., *Key Data on Adolescence* (Brighton: Trust for the Study of Adolescence, 1997).

Domestic Food Consumption and Expenditure, 1950, Report of the National Food Survey Committee, 1952.

Education and Training Statistics for the United Kingdom 1998 (London: DEE, SO, 1998).

Family Spending, A Report on the 1997–98 Family Expenditure Survey (London: ONS, SO, 1998).

Gallup Report, *British Attitudes Towards the Common Market 1957* (London: 1971).

Hayward, B., Taylor, S., Smith, N. and Davis, G., *Evaluation of the Campaign for Older Workers* (London: DEE, 1997).

Higher Education, Report of the Committee Appointed by the Prime Minister under the Chairmanship of Lord Robbins 1961–1963, Cmnd 2154 (London: HMSO, 1963).

The Impact of Large Food Stores on Market Towns and District Centres (London: DETR, SO, 1998).

Ministry of Education, 'Maintained and Assisted Primary and Secondary Schools', *Stats Return*, January 1955.

Mintel, *1998 British Lifestyles* (London: Mintel International, 1998).

Mirrlees-Black, C. and Budd, T., *Policing and the Public: Findings from the 1996 British Crime Survey*, Home Office Research and Statistics Directorate, *Research Findings* no. 60, pp. 1–2.

Social Focus on Ethnic Minorities (London: HMSO, 1996).

Social Focus on Families (London: ONS, SO, 1997).

Social Focus on Older People (London: ONS, SO, 1999).

Social Focus on the Unemployed (London: ONS, SO, 1998).

Social Focus on Women (London: CSO, HMSO, 1995).

Social Focus on Women and Men (London: ONS, SO, 1998).

Articles

Atkinson, A. B., 'Seeking to Explain the Distribution of Income' in J. Hills (ed.), *New Inequalities the Changing Distribution of Income and Wealth in the United Kingdom* (Cambridge: Cambridge University Press, 1996).

Ballard, R., 'Differentiation and Disjunction and the Sikhs' in Ballard, *Desh Pardesh*.

Berrington, A., 'Marriage Patterns and Inter-ethnic Unions' in Coleman and Salt, *Ethnicity*, vol. 1.

Blackburn, R. M. and Jarman, J., 'Changing Inequalities in Access to British Universities', *Oxford Review of Education*, vol. 19, no. 2, 1993, pp. 197–215.

Brook, L., 'The Public Response to AIDS' in R. Jowell *et al.*, *British Social Attitudes 5th Report, 1988*.

Brown, R. and Julius, D., 'Is Manufacturing Still Special?' in *The Amex Bank Review*, vol. 20, no. 9, 1993, pp. 2–3.

Bruce, S. and Alderdice, F., 'Religious Belief and Behaviour' in *Social Attitudes in Northern Ireland, 1992–93* (Belfast: Blackstaff, 1993).

Cannadine, D., 'The British Monarchy and the Invention of Tradition c. 1820–1977' in Hobsbawm and Ranger, *The Invention of Tradition*.

Cohen, R., 'Fuzzy Frontiers of Identity: The British Case' *Social Identities*, vol. 1, no. 1, 1995.

M. Collins, 'Who Voted What' in Jowell and Hoinville (eds), *Britain Into Europe*.

Commager, H. S., 'English Traits, One Hundred Years Later' in *The Nineteenth Century*, July 1948 as reprinted in Commager, (ed.), *Britain Through American Eyes*.

Crompton, R., 'Where Did All the Bright Girls Go? Women's Higher Education and Employment Since 1964' in Abercrombie and Warde, *Social Change in Contemporary Britain*.

Curtice, J., 'Political Sociology 1945–92' in Obelkevich and Catterall (eds), *Understanding Post-War British Society*.

Davies, K. S., Walker, P. and Tupman, D., 'Universities, Numbers, Money and Policies, 1945–85' in Stewart, *Higher Education in Postwar Britain*.

Derbyshire, A., 'Building the Welfare State' in B. Goldstein (ed.), *Architecture: Opportunities, Achievements*, a report of the Annual Conference of the Royal Institute of British Architects held at the University of Hull, 14 to 17 July 1976 (London: 1977).

Desai, T., Gregg, P., Steer, J. and Wadsworth, J., 'Gender and the Labour Market' in Gregg and Wadsworth, *The State of Working Britain*.

Disney, R., 'Why Have Older Men Stopped Working?' in Gregg and Wadsworth, *The State of Working Britain*.

Eade, J., Vamplew, T. and Peach, C. 'The Bangladeshis: The Encapsulated Community' in Peach, *Ethnicity*, vol. 2.

Egerton, M. and Halsey, A. H., 'Trends by Social Class and Gender in Access to Higher Education in Britain', *Oxford Review of Education*, vol. 19, no. 2, 1993, pp. 183–96.

Elliot, B. J., 'Demographic Trends in Domestic Life, 1945–87' in Clark (ed.), *Marriage, Domestic Life and Social Change*.

Farrelly, E. M., 'The Venturi Effect', *The Architectural Review*, no. 1084, June 1987, pp. 32–7.

Field, C. D. 'The Secularised Sabbath Revisited: Opinion Polls as Sources for Sunday Observance in Contemporary Britain', *Contemporary British History*, vol. 15, no. 1, London, spring 2001.

Gardner, K. and Shukar, A., 'I'm Bengali, I'm Asian and I'm Living Here' in Ballard, *Desh Pardesh*.

Gerbet, P., 'La Genese du Plan Schuman', *Revue Francaise de Science Politique*, vol. 6, no. 3 (Paris, July–September 1956).

Gorling, A., Machin, S. and Meghir, C., 'What Has Happened to the Wages of Men Since 1966?' in Hills (ed.), *New Inequalities: The Changing Distribution of Income and Wealth in the United Kingdom*.

Halsey, A. H., 'Further and Higher Education' in Halsey and Webb, *Twentieth-Century British Social Trends*.

Harding, S., 'Trends in Permissiveness' in Jowell *et al.*, *British Social Attitudes 5th Report, 1988*.

Harkness, S., 'The Gender Earnings Gap: Evidence from the U.K.' *Fiscal Studies*, vol. 17, no. 2, 1996, pp. 3–35.

Heath, A. and Park, A., 'Thatcher's Children?' in *British Social Attitudes, 14th Report, 1997–98.*

Hinds, K. and Jarvis, L. 'The Gender Gap' in *British Social Attitudes 17th Report, 2000–2001.*

Hirst, P. H., 'The Foundations of the National Curriculum: Why Subjects?' in O'Hear and White, *Assessing the National Curriculum.*

Johnson, A. M. *et al.*, 'Sexual Behaviour in Britain: Partnerships, Practices and HIV Risk Behaviour', *The Lancet*, 1 December 2001.

Kohli, M., 'Work and Retirement: A Comparative Perspective' in Riley, Kahn and Foner (eds), *Age and Structural Lag.*

Lewis, P. 'Being Muslim and Being British' in Ballard, *Desh Pardesh.*

Modood, T., 'The Number of Ethnic Minority Students in British Higher Education: Some Grounds for Optimism', *Oxford Review of Education*, vol. 19, no. 2, 1993, pp. 167–81.

Modood, T., 'Qualifications and English Language' in Modood and Berthoud, *Ethnic Minorities.*

Nugent, N., 'British Public Opinion and the European Community' in George (ed.), *Britain and the European Community.*

Price, R. and Baine, G. S., 'The Labour Force' in Halsey (ed.), *British Social Trends Since 1900.*

Raven, J., 'British History and the Enterprise Culture', *Past and Present*, no. 123, May 1989, pp. 178–204.

Royle, E., 'Trends in Post-War British Social History' in Obelkevich and Catterall, *Understanding.*

Slessor, C., 'Oxford Ordonnance' in *Architectural Review*, vol. 196, no. 1172, 1994, pp. 43–9.

Stamp. G., 'How Hillingdon Happened', *Architectural Review*, no. 984, 1979, pp. 85–91.

Strinati, D., 'Postmodernism and Popular Culture', *Sociology Review*, vol. 1, no. 4, 1992, pp. 2–7.

Summerfield, P., 'Women in Britain Since 1945' in Obelkevich and Catterall, *Understanding.*

Tarling, R. and Dowds, L., 'Crime and Punishment' in *British Social Attitudes*, 14th Report, 1997–98.

Taylor, P., 'Access to Higher Education: An Uneven Path?' in Goulbourne and Lewis-Meeks (eds), *Access of Ethnic Minorities to Higher Education in Britain*, Centre for Research in Ethnic Relations, Occasional Papers in Ethnic Relations, no. 10 (Warwick: 1993).

Thane, P., 'Towards Equal Opportunities? Women in Britain Since 1945' in Gourvish and O'Day (eds), *Britain Since 1945.*

Tinker, A., 'Old Age and Gerontology' in Obelkevich and Catterall, *Understanding.*

Tiratsoo, N., 'Limits of Americanisation: The United States Productivity Gospel in Britain' in Conekin, Mort and Waters, C. (eds), *Moments of Modernity.*

Toland, S., 'Changes in Living Standards Since the 1950s' in *Social Trends 1980*, pp. 13–38.

Waters, C., 'J. B. Priestley 1894–1984' in Pedersen and Mandler (eds), *After the Victorians.*

Wellings, K. *et al.*, 'Sexual Behaviour in Britain: Early Heterosexual Experience', *The Lancet*, 1 December 2001.

Willcock, H. D., 'Public Opinion: Attitudes Towards America and Russia', *The Political Quarterly*, vol. 19, no. 1 (London: 1948).

Young, K., 'Class, Race and Opportunity' in *British Social Attitudes*, 9th Report, 1992.

Books

Abercrombie, N. and Warde, A., *Social Change in Contemporary Britain* (Cambridge: Polity Press, 1992).

Abrams, M., Gerard, D. and Timms, N. (eds), *Values and Social Change in Britain* (Basingstoke: Macmillan, 1985).

Adonis, A. and Pollard, S., *A Class Act* (London: Hamish Hamilton, 1997).

Amery, C., *A Celebration of Art and Architecture* (London: National Gallery, 1991).

Ballard, R. (ed.), *Desh Pardesh: The South Asian Presence in Britain* (London: Hurst, 1994).

Barker, E., *The Common Market* (London: G. P. Putnam, 1973).

Beloff, Lord, *Britain and European Union* (Basingstoke: Macmillan, 1996).

Benn, C. and Chitty, C., *Thirty Years On Is Comprehensive Education Alive and Well or Struggling to Survive?* (London: David Fulton, 1996).

Bogdanor, V., *The Monarchy and the Constitution* (Oxford: Clarendon Press, 1995).

Brown, C. G., *The Death of Christian Britain* (London: Routledge, 2001).

Bruce, S., *Religion in Modern Britain* (Oxford: Oxford University Press, 1995).

Burnett, J., *Idle Hands: The Experience of Unemployment 1790–1990* (London: Routledge, 1994).

Burnett, J., *Plenty and Want: A Social History of Diet in England from 1815 to the Present Day* (London: Routledge, 1989).

Burnett, J., *A Social History of Housing 1815–1985* (London: Routledge,1986).

Butler, D. and Kitzinger, U.W., *The 1975 Referendum* (London: Macmillan, 1976).

Callaghan, J., *Time and Chance* (London: Collins, 1988).

Cannadine, D., *Class in Britain* (New Haven:Yale University Press, 1998).

The Carnegie Inquiry into theThirdAge, Final Report: Life,Work and Livelihood in theThirdAge (Dunfermline: Carnegie United KingdomTrust, 1993).

Chase, M. E., *In England Now* (London: Collins, 1937).

Clark, D. (ed.), *Marriage, Domestic Life and Social Change* (London: Routledge, 1991).

Cohen, R., *Frontiers of Identity: The British and the Others* (London: Longman,1994).

Coleman, D. and Salt, J. (eds), *Ethnicity in the 1991 Census*, vol. 1 (London: HMSO, 1996).

Collins, B. and Robbins K. (eds), *British Culture and Economic Decline* (London:Weidenfeld and Nicolson, 1990).

Commager, H. S. (ed.), *Britain through American Eyes* (London: Bodley Head, 1974).

Conekin, B., Mort, F. andWaters, C. (eds), *Moments of Modernity* (London: Rivers Oram, 1999).

Crook, J. M., *The Dilemma of Style* (London: Murray, 1987).

David, E., *A Book of Mediterranean Food* (London: Dorling Kindersley, 1950).

Davie, G., *Religion in Britain Since 1945* (Oxford: Blackwell, 1994).

Dimbleby, D. and Reynolds, D., *An Ocean Apart* (London: Hodder and Stoughton, 1988).

Dimbleby, J., *The Prince ofWales* (London: Little Brown, 1994).

Driver, C., *The British at Table* (London: Hogarth Press, 1983).

Edmunds, R., *Setting the Mould* (Oxford: Clarendon Press, 1986).

Ellis,W., *The Oxbridge Conspiracy* (London: Michael Joseph, 1994).

Fielding, S., *Labour: Decline and Renewal* (Manchester: Baseline, 1995).

Floud, R. and McCloskey, D. (eds), *The Economic History of Britain Since 1700*, vol. 3, *1939–1992* (Cambridge: Cambridge University Press, 1994).

Frith, S., *The Sociology ofYouth* (Ormskirk: Causeway Books, 1984).

George, S., *An Awkward Partner: Britain in the European Community* (Oxford: Oxford University Press, 1990).

George, S. (ed.), *Britain and the European Community* (Oxford: Clarendon Press, 1992).

Gillis, J. R., *Youth and History* (London: Academic Press, 1981).

Glancey, J., *New British Architecture* (London: Thames and Hudson, 1989).

Glendinning, M. and Muthesius, S., *Tower Block* (New Haven: Yale University Press, 1994).

Gorer, G., *Exploring English Character* (London: Cresset Press, 1955).

Goulbourne, H. and Lewis-Meeks, P. (eds), *Access of Ethnic Minorities to Higher Education in Britain* (Warwick: University of Warwick, 1993).

Gourvish, T. and O'Day, A. (eds), *Britain Since 1945* (Basingstoke: Macmillan, 1991).

Gowland, P. and Turner, A., *Reluctant Europeans* (Harlow: Longman, 2000).

Gregg, P. and Wadsworth, J., *The State of Working Britain* (Manchester: Manchester University Press, 1999).

Halsey, A. H. (ed.), *British Social Trends Since 1900* (Basingstoke: Macmillan, 1988).

Halsey, A. H., *Change in British Society* (Oxford: Oxford University Press, 1995).

Halsey, A. H. and Webb, J., *Twentieth-Century British Social Trends* (Basingstoke: Macmillan, 2000).

Harris, L. M., *Long To Reign Over Us? The Status of the Royal Family in the Sixties* (London: Kimber, 1966).

Heath, A. F., Jowell, R. and Curtice, J., *How Britain Votes* (Oxford: Pergamon, 1985).

Heath, A. F., *Understanding Political Change* (Oxford: Pergamon, 1991).

Hessayon, D. G., *The Rose Expert* (Waltham Cross: pbi publications, 1988).

Hewison, R., *The Heritage Industry* (London: Methuen, 1987).

Hills, J. (ed.), *New Inequalities: The Changing Distribution of Income and Wealth in the United Kingdom* (Cambridge: Cambridge University Press, 1996).

Hobsbawm, E. and Ranger, T., *The Invention of Tradition* (Cambridge: Cambridge University Press, 1983).

Hoggart, R., *The Uses of Literacy* (London: Chatto and Windus, 1957).

Hollowell, J., *Britain Since 1945* (Oxford: Blackwell, 2003).

Holmes, C., *A Tolerant Country? Immigrants, Refugees and Minorities in Britain* (London: Faber, 1991).

Hopkins, E., *The Rise and Decline of the English Working Classes 1918–1990* (London: Weidenfield and Nicolson, 1991).

Hopkins, H., *The New Look* (London: Readers Union, 1964).

Jackson, A., *The Politics of Architecture* (London: Architectural Publishers, 1970).

Jacobs, E. and Worcester, R., *Typically British?* (London: Bloomsbury, 1991).

Jefferys, M. (ed.), *Growing Old in the Twentieth Century* (London: Routledge, 1989).

Jencks, C., *Architecture Today* (London: Academy Editions, 1993).

Jencks, C., *What Is Post-Modernism?* (London: Academy Editions, 1989).

Jenkins, S., *Accountable to None* (London: Hamish Hamilton, 1995).

Johnson, P. (ed.), *Twentieth-Century Britain* (London: Longman, 1994).

Jones, G. and Wallace, C., *Youth, Family and Citizenship* (Buckingham: Open University Press, 1992).

Jowell, R. and Hoinville, G. (eds), *Britain Into Europe* (London: Croom Helm, 1976).

Jowell, R. and Spence, J., *The Grudging Europeans: A Study of British Attitudes towards the EEC* (London: Social and Community Planning Research, Centre for Sample Surveys, 1975).

Kerckhoff, A., Fogelman, K., Crook, D. and Reeder, D., *Going Comprehensive in England and Wales* (London: Woburn Press, 1996).

King, A., *Britain Says Yes* (Washington: American Enterprise Institute for Public Policy Research, 1977).

Larkin, P., *High Windows* (London: Faber and Faber, 1974).

Laslett, P., *A Fresh Map of Life* (London: Macmillan, 1996).

Lazard, R., King, J. and Morse, C., *The Impact of Robbins* (Harmondsworth: Penguin, 1969).

Lewis, J., *Women in Britain Since 1945* (Oxford: Blackwell, 1992).

Lowe, J., *Giving and Inheriting* (London: Which?, 1994).

Marshall, G., Newby, H., Rose, D. and Vogler, C., *Social Class in Modern Britain* (London: Hutchinson, 1988).

Marwick, A., *Britain in the Century of Total War* (London: Bodley Head, 1968).

Marwick, A., *British Society Since 1945* (London: Penguin, 1996).

Mason, D., *Race and Ethnicity in Modern Britain* (Oxford: Oxford University Press, 1995).

McConnell, J., *English Public Schools* (London: Herbert Press, 1985).

McKibbin, R., *Classes and Cultures England 1918–1951* (Oxford: Oxford University Press, 1998).

Melly, G., *Revolt Into Style* (London: Allen Lane, 1970).

Modood, T., *Ethnic Minorities and Higher Education* (London: Policy Studies Institute, 1994).

Modood, T. and Berthoud, R. (eds), *Ethnic Minorities in Britain* (London: Policy Studies Institute, 1997).

Morgan, K. O., *Britain Since 1945* (Oxford: Oxford University Press, 2001).

Morgan, K. O., *Labour in Power, 1945–51* (Oxford: Clarendon Press, 1984).

Mort, F., *Cultures of Consumption* (London: Routledge, 1996).

Nuttgens, P., *The Home Front* (London: BBC, 1989).

Nuttgens, P., *Understanding Modern Architecture* (London: Unwin Hyman, 1988).

Obelkevich, J. and Catterall, P., *Understanding Post-War British Society* (London: Routledge, 1994).

O'Hear, P. and White, J., *Assessing the National Curriculum* (London: Paul Chapman, 1993).

Orwell, G., *The Lion and the Unicorn* (1941) (Harmondsworth: Penguin Books, 1982).

Osborne, J., *Look Back in Anger* (1957) (London: Faber and Faber, 1996).

Osgerby, B., *Youth in Britain Since 1945* (Oxford: Blackwell, 1998).

Paxman, J., *Friends in High Places: Who Runs Britain* (London: Penguin, 1990).

Peach, C. (ed.), *Ethnicity in the 1991 Census*, vol. 2 (London: HMSO, 1996).

Pedersen, S. and Mandler, P. (eds), *After theVictorians* (London: Routledge, 1994).

Pelling, H., *A History of British Trade Unionism* (Basingstoke: Macmillan, 1992).

Pelling, H. and Reid, A. J., *A Short History of the Labour Party* (Basingstoke: Macmillan,1996).

Pilcher, J., *Age and Generation in Modern Britain* (Oxford: Oxford University Press, 1995).

Postgate, J. and M., *A Stomach for Dissent: The Life of Raymond Postgate 1896–1971* (Keele: Keele University Press, 1994).

Priestley, J. B., *English Journey* (1934) (London: Heinemann, 1984).

Priestley, J. B. and Hawkes, J., *Journey Down a Rainbow* (London: Reader's Union, 1957).

Prochaska, F., *Royal Bounty* (New Haven: Yale University Press, 1995).

Reid, I., *Class in Britain* (Cambridge: Polity Press, 1998).

Reid, I., *Social Class Differences in Britain* (London: Fontana, 1989).

Riley, M.W., Kahn, R. L. and Foner, A. (eds), *Age and Structural Lag* (New York: Wiley, 1994).

Ring, A., *The Story of Princess Elizabeth* (London: Murray, 1930).

Rogers, R., *Architecture: A Modern View* (London: Thames and Hudson, 1990).

Rubinstein, W. D., *Capitalism, Culture and Decline in Britain 1750–1990* (London: Routledge, 1993).

Saint, A., *Towards a Social Architecture* (New Haven: Yale University Press, 1987).

Sampson, A., *The Essential Anatomy of Britain* (London: Hodder and Stoughton, 1992).

Samuel, R., *Theatres of Memory*, vol. 1 (London: Verso, 1994).

Sanderson, M., *Education and Economic Decline in Britain, 1870 to the 1990s* (Cambridge: Cambridge University Press, 1999).

Sargant, N., *The Learning Divide* (Leicester: NIACE, 1997).

Seymour-Ure, C., *The British Press and Broadcasting Since 1945* (Oxford: Blackwell, 1991).

Shepherd, R.J., *Public Opinion and European Integration* (Farnborough: Lexington Books, 1975).

Sked, A., *Britain's Decline* (Oxford: Basil Blackwell, 1987).

Simon, B., *Education and the Social Order, 1940–1990* (London: Lawrence and Wishart, 1991).

Smith. D., *North and South* (London: Penguin, 1989).

Snowman, D., *Kissing Cousins* (London: Temple Smith, 1977).

Stewart, W. A. C., *Higher Education in Postwar Britain* (Basingstoke: Macmillan, 1989).

Sudjic, D., *The Architecture of Richard Rogers* (London: Fourth Estate and Wordsearch, 1994).

Sudjic, D., *Norman Foster, Richard Rogers, James Stirling* (London: Thames and Hudson, 1986).

Taylor, R., *The Trade Union Question in British Politics* (Oxford: Blackwell, 1998).

Thane, P., *Old Age in English History* (Oxford: Oxford University Press, 2000).

Thompson, P., Itzin, C. and Abendstern, M., *I Don't Feel Old* (Oxford: Oxford University Press, 1991).

Tomlinson, R., *Divine Right: The Inglorious Survival of British Royalty* (London: Abacus, 1995).

Victor, C. R., *Old Age in Modern Society* (London: Chapman and Hall, 1994).

HRH the Prince of Wales, *A Vision of Britain* (London: Doubleday, 1989).

Walford, G., *Life in Public Schools* (London: Methuen, 1986).

Walford, G., *Privatisation and Privilege in Education* (London: Routledge, 1990).

Warde. A. and Abercrombie, N. (eds), *Stratification and Social Inequality* (Lancaster: Framework, 1994).

Weeks, J., *Coming Out* (London: Quartet Books, 1990).

Wellings, K., Field, J., Johnson, A. and Wadsworth, J., *Sexual Behaviour in Britain* (London: Penguin, 1994).

Wiener, M., *English Culture and the Decline of the Industrial Spirit 1850–1980* (Cambridge: Cambridge University Press, 1981).

Williams, F., *The American Invasion* (London: A. Blond, 1962).

Wood, M., *America in the Movies* (New York: Columbia University Press, 1989).

Young, H., *This Blessed Plot* (London: Macmillan, 1998).

Ziegler, P., *Crown and People* (London: Collins, 1978).

Miscellaneous

MacCormac, R., 'Architecture, History and Narrative', a lecture given at Oxford University Department for Continuing Education, 11 February 1997.

Winchester College, 'Notions' (pamphlet), Winchester, n.d.

Index

Printed in the United Kingdom
by Lightning Source UK Ltd.
132948UK00001B/241-276/P